GW00322447

GOOD AND HEALTHY

COLIN SPENCER

GOOD AND HEALTHY

A Vegetarian and Wholefood Cookbook

Robson Books

First published in Great Britain in 1983 by Robson Books Ltd,
Bolsover House, 5–6 Clipstone Street, London W1P 7EB
This Robson paperback edition first published 1990

British Library Cataloguing in Publication Data

Spencer, Colin
  Good and healthy.
  1. Vegetarians. Food: Dishes using natural food. Recipes
  I. Title
  641.5'636

  ISBN 0 86051 648 2

Printed in Hungary

Contents

Preface

Preface to the paperback edition

The present book absorbed and reflected many of my *Guardian* articles printed seven years ago. How these came to be written is explained in the introduction. Ideologically, the words written then need to be emphasized with greater solemnity now. It is clear that the need for a vegetarian and humanitarian lifestyle today is all the more urgent. For this has come to be seen rightly as the green or environmental way of coping with the modern world, of stemming the tidal wave of pollution, even though it often feels like a Canute gesture. So, though I stand by every word I wrote then I think the enemy now can be identified with more accuracy.

It is a modern tragedy that the powers behind the world food supply have become centred more and more in the hands of a monopoly of four or five giant multinationals. These embrace the pharmaceutical industry, they control the variety of seeds and which pesticides they will genetically favour to the selective breeding of livestock, as well as the canning, freezing, processing and distribution of food. Technology on the farm and in the factory where the ingredients are mangled, tumbled, pumped full of water, air and chemicals, has become so sophisticated that it can look beguiling while having few actual nutrients. Thus it is food which is a snare for the busy family, also this kind of processed junk is very addictive for young children. All the more reason then to stick to the fresh raw ingredients which these pages celebrate.

The horrors of factory intensive farming are now more widely known. We now have evidence of the diseases which flourish in closed housing units and how livestock is kept alive until the time of slaughter by massive and daily doses of antibiotics. We have experienced countless food poisoning outbreaks which will continue until the gross anomaly of factory farms are abolished. This is one essential windmill which the vegetarian Don Quixote tilts at. But you don't even have to be a pure vegetarian in order to put pressure upon intensive farmers to change over to free-range systems. You can instead be an occasional consumer of free-range meat, for more and more farmers are now moving to organic and free-range systems. The trend has begun, the rest of the Nineties will see it intensify.

Unfortunately the pollution of our land with pesticides and nitrates has grown. It is estimated that if farmers stopped pouring nitrate fertilizer into the soil now, it would be 30 to 40 years before our water supply was free of the contaminants. These affect vegetables and fruits, we are not allowed to see Government research into pesticide residues in the vegetables on sale to the public. Nor do retailers publicize their findings. This, of course, makes us suspicious. There is no Freedom of Information Act in the UK so we can still be giving our children food which is contaminated with chemicals while the Government fails to warn us in time. Consumers have enormous potential power and there are now new bodies-like Parents for Safe Food which are lobbying Government for new protective legislation.

Washing fruit and vegetables under cold running water does not always eradicate a pesticide. If it is systemic, the plant has taken it up in its own cell structure, so buy organic wherever possible. The more the consumer buys organic produce the greater the amount that will be produced. Recently, after long delays and urgent lobbying, the Government has agreed to subsidize the organic farmer while he changes over from chemical farming.

There are, there is little doubt, these small signs of hope. We are changing our ways, slowly we are learning to respect other life on this planet, learning not to exploit living animals for the food we do not need, for a diet based on plants is more than adequate for our health and well-being. Slowly we are learning to see the world as a whole, as an intricate web, the chain of being which man must respect and never tamper with. But the future is fraught, genetic engineering of both plants and animals has begun and the next decade will see the products of it. So we who suspect that this is inherently wrong must be all the more active and watchful in our attempt to protect the context in which we live.

More aware too of the animals with which we share our living space, these animals which we have tortured and abused in the name of efficient food production; the world is slowly now becoming aware of Henry Beston's words: 'They are not brethren; they are not underlings; they are other nations, caught with ourselves in the net of life and time, fellow prisoners of the splendour and travail of the earth.'

Introduction

This book is based on my articles which have been appearing in the *Guardian* since 1979. I am indebted to that newspaper, and to Liz Forgan who was then editor of the Women's Page, for asking me to write an 'alternative' food column. I am also grateful to Jill Tweedie and to Polly Toynbee, who insisted that such a column discussed the food of the future and that no responsible newspaper should ignore it.

The *Guardian* in fact is unique, for there is no other national daily newspaper in the world which runs a food column that is vegetarian and whole-food (not always the same), that attempts the difficult balance between being gourmet and healthy, that gives information about nutrition, and that attempts to attack the vested interests which monopolize the food industry.

Food is vital, the most basic commodity in the world. The lack of it is used as a form of torture or of self-martyrdom, while the preparation of it is extolled as an art form. Food (or its lack) can be used as political blackmail to subjugate under-developed countries. The richer countries use food supply as a persuasive tactic to keep their favoured regimes in power in lesser countries. While millions die from diseases associated with a lack of food (what food there is is poor in quality), in the richest third of the world people die from diseases associated with too rich a diet, a surfeit of fats and sugars. Government subsidies ensure that the rich stay rich. Mountains of food

12

are allowed to rot away under EEC food policies. All this is common knowledge, yet the media on the whole tend to dispense food information to the public concerned with the social trivia of dinner parties.

I have tried to find a diet which respects humanity and life. I have also tried to think of food in a world context, to eat that which is good but the eating of which cannot harm others. Yet I have been forced to admit that this is an impossible ideal — the food industry exploits world labour, pays it a pittance and feeds the labour force on scraps.

Could Dr Johnson have been right, 'That a man would rather kill a cow than not eat beef?' I think not; if we all had to kill the animal itself before we cooked and ate it, the majority of us would be vegetarian. It is unnecessary to kill animals to survive. By avoiding eating animal flesh you are not causing the suffering inherent in factory farming and the slaughter house, and you are not eating food that might harm you (residual antibiotics, commercial additives and chemicals). A vegetarian diet is almost certainly a far healthier one; what research there is on vegetarians has concluded that they are less prone to the most common diseases which afflict the industrial countries.

This book, then, is dedicated to promoting food which is good, and healthy.

What is a Healthy Diet

We have one of the highest heart disease death rates in the world. It is the most frequent cause of death in middle-aged men and the death rate is also rising in women. Indeed half of all deaths are caused by heart disease. Most of these premature deaths could be prevented by changing our life style — and especially our diet. But improving our diet is made harder by the fact that no law exists which requires manufacturers to tell the consumer how much fat or sugar is added to foods.

We do not ask what the fat content is in digestive biscuits, or cream crackers, or even breakfast cereals, but if we did we might find it alarming. We know there is quite a bit of fat in sausages, but frankfurters always look rather lean and slim. In fact, they contain slightly more fat than pork sausages. There is also some fat and sugar in tinned soups, vegetables and baked beans; and here I mention only a very few foods which many of us eat daily.

Food manufacturers excuse the lack of information by saying that consumers would not know how to use it. But behind this tiresome attitude there surely lurks the suspicion that if we had such facts we would be more particular about buying a product.

While most information is omitted, what little there is can be confusing. Take, for example, 'blended vegetable oils,' which appears on some margarine and cooking oils. The label says nothing about saturated or polyunsaturated fats and because of the word 'vegetable' one is inclined to think it is not saturated fat. But a product made of 'blended vegetable oils' will almost certainly contain palm or coconut oil which is high in saturated fats.

The recent advertising battle between butter and margarine exploited public confusion. But as butter sales have fallen steadily for many years, fogging the issues may help the Butter Council to claw back a chunk of the market. (In the last months of 1980 margarine sales beat sales of butter for the first time since 1956.) When butter accounts for so much of the saturated fat in our diet, such tactics could appear irresponsible.

It is possible to change our diet. In the early Sixties the US statistics for coronary heart disease were among the highest in the world. Since then they have fallen by 25 per cent to below our own. A US Department of Agriculture survey on a random sample of the population discovered that about half had changed their eating habits for health reasons. The Department also found that sales of milk, butter, eggs and lard had all fallen, while sales of low-fat yoghurt, cottage cheese and margarine had doubled.

In Britain, the Coronary Prevention Group (CPG) has recently been formed to help us change our eating patterns. The group points out that over the last 30 years we have eaten less starchy carbohydrates, but steadily consumed more fat, more sugar and more alcohol.

We each get through an amazing 100 g/4 oz of fat per day. One third of that comes from dairy produce (butter, milk, cream, cheese), one third from meat and its products (sausages, pies, burgers, salamis and potted pastes) and one third from margarine and cooking fats in cakes and biscuits. In the north and in Scotland we eat more animal fat, simply because the cheaper cuts of meat are used in cooking.

The good news is that the change in lifestyle which the CPG would like to see is not a huge one. We must watch how much fat and sugar we are consuming daily and cut it by a quarter, while the saturated fats should be cut by a half. But if a product has fat added to it and is not clearly marked as such, that is impossible without refusing all commercial food products altogether.

The reduction in fats places the cookery writer in somewhat of a quandary. How much butter, cream or cheese can I responsibly put into a list of ingredients? Only half of what I might have been cooking with before. But it would seem to me that I can also search for alternatives which taste as good. I have long known skimmed milk (which can now be bought in liquid form) is far better for the classic white sauces. I have also enjoyed using yoghurt in Middle Eastern recipes. The CPG points out that coronary heart diseases are low in all the Mediterranean countries and in the Far East.

If we stand in our kitchen flanked by large tins of olive oil and ropes of garlic on one side and a wok and packets of tofu on the other we will not go far wrong. We must also eat more good quality bread, more pasta, potatoes, rice and dried beans, which are not fattening, the CPG claims, if not eaten with fats.

If this sounds dull, I would argue it need not be. Sauces can be made with a base of olive oil, yoghurt and low fat cheeses. All the countries with a minimal fat consumption also use spices and herbs with great skill. And if we knew from glancing at a label what exactly we were eating, we could really hope to control our diet, which also happens to be our life and death.

Vegetarians are fortunate. The third of saturated fat that comes from meat and its products, they avoid. Also their diet is naturally high in fibre, because they consume more raw vegetables, more cooked vegetables in their skins, more bran, cereals and wholemeal bread.

Dr Denis Burkitt, an authority on fibre, claims that the excreta of vegetarians is by far the healthiest: stools should be fairly soft and fall lightly into a pyramid shape. Compact stools are not a sign of a healthy diet.

It is not only coronary heart disease which is affected by a change of diet, reducing the number of deaths and

16

preventing the arteries from clotting, but over twenty other diseases which are rife in our society can be influenced by the same change of diet. Preventive medicine claims that we would be entirely free of these diseases if we ate such a diet from the earliest age. They are tooth decay, strokes, intestinal disorders, such as diverticulitis, appendicitis, piles and constipation, breast and colon cancers, diabetes mellitis, gallstones and, of course, obesity.

SUGAR

Surely everyone by now knows that sugar is bad for us. Food manufacturers know that sugar is bad for us, but they continue to add sugar to foods. Health and wholefood shops know that sugar is bad for us, but they stock brown sugars. And nearly all of us eat sugar of one colour or another.

Behind the double-think there is also confusion. A health-food booklet, *Sugarless Desserts*, suggests making them with maple syrup — seemingly unaware that it is sucrose and water. We think of honey as healthier than sugar, yet honey is fructose and glucose, a form called invert sugar, which is just as harmful. We think of all the brown sugars as being better for us than white sugar, but it is untrue.

All sugars are cariogenic. In other words, all sugars, as well as honey and maple syrup, treacles and molasses, are the prime cause of dental decay and gum disease.

Do not be taken in by brown sugars calling themselves raw and unrefined, making claims of health and naturalness. All sugar is refined. It has to be — otherwise you would be left with a stick of cane or a lump of beet.

In Britain only three out of a thousand adults have never experienced dental disease. Eighty per cent of six-year-old children suffer from decay and ninety-seven per cent of fifteen-year-olds. Dental treatment costs the health service £124 million per year, and that is a modest estimate. We are, in fact, so used to this epidemic of caries that we just take it for granted, rather like living with the bomb. You might think we could dig in our heels and call a halt now.

Sugar is also a powerful contributory factor in obesity, diabetes and heart disease, as well as other diseases of the digestive system. We eat on average 100 g/4 oz of sugar per day. The amount we consume soared from the beginning of the century (jam being much cheaper than butter for smearing on bread) and declined only in the war years when it was rationed.

We are aware of the sugar added to cups of tea or coffee, or sprinkled on breakfast cereals, the sugar in preserves, cakes, pastries and biscuits — visible sugar, if you like. But there is, too, the invisible sugar which is added by the food manufacturers to diverse items like canned soups and pickles. Even more sugar seems to be added now to savoury foods: liver pâté and sausages, sliced ham or corned beef, frozen beef patties, pies and burgers, frozen fish cakes and potted salmon, dried meals and frozen vegetables. It appears to be the most widely used additive of all.

The idea that sugar gives you energy is much loved by television advertising, where we are begged to chew or crunch at choc bars of sticky goo to give us strength, while at the same time there is flashed on the screen an image of a trim waistline.

Sugar is what is known as an empty calorie, a food without nutrients. It is an unnecessary component in the diet as it tends to replace other foods which have fibre, minerals and vitamins. The idea that sugar gives you energy is only true in the sense that all food gives you energy. The idea may have gained credence from sportsmen who take glucose tablets before running. But they chose glucose instead of two pieces of wholemeal bread, so that they could run and not have to stop and sit on the loo.

There are sugars, of course, in both fruits and vegetables. But you would have to eat twenty apples in order to consume 100 g/4 oz of sugar and in the fruit you have fibre and nutrients. Dried fruit condenses both the sugars and the fibre; it requires chewing, which produces saliva, and as that is alkaline it protects against caries.

Rewards, treats or bribes for children need not centre around confectionery. Try and make other foods desirable. Parents-to-be are the most vulnerable citizens of all, for though Health Education and Dental Health and Hospital booklets abound in dietary advice, they seem to draw back from spelling it out. They never tell you to avoid all sugars like the plague.

There are other booklets, published by the British Sugar Bureau, the Chocolate, Cocoa and Confectionery Alliance, and Mars Limited, which are to say the least prejudiced on the subject. *My Tooth Diary*, brought out by Mars Limited and — wait for it — the General Dental Council, fails to mention sugar at all but gives the impression that all will be well as long as you brush your teeth.

The nearest it gets to the truth is when it says: 'Food left on your teeth helps germs to attack your teeth.' Perhaps the sponsors were hoping that we might be under the impression celery or cheese, and not sugar, would give us dental decay.

All the vested interests tend to give large amounts of money towards research. They are attempting to discover a vaccine agains caries at the moment, but it will be a long time before an injection can protect a child's teeth. Naturally, in this research you have to get the monkeys started off on the road to rotting teeth. So what do you think they are fed on? Just some of that confectionery goo that is advertised on television. It seems cruel to the monkeys, but vested interests in the sugar lobby are a powerful bunch.

Avoiding sugar is as much social as dietetic. The cake is still considered a celebration food. Afternoon tea may be on the decline but it still exists. Marmalade and jams are made. Fresh fruits are sprinkled with caster sugar. The pudding is still considered to be *de rigeur* for a dinner party. The dessert trolley at restaurants is laden with platters piled high with whipped cream and sugared fruits.

Sugar has become in fact a central part of the gloss of high living: we feel that without it a proper meal is not complete.

Because of this we have to re-educate ourselves. Sugar is unnecessary in our diet. We must do all that we can to avoid it. The worst and most agonizing problem is for parents of young children. Not only is there the barrage of television advertising, but our whole social system works on sweet bribes and sweet treats in a childhood environment. But to be aware of it is taking the first step towards fighting the influence.

FATS

Early in 1982 there opened a two-day international seminar at the Royal College of Physicians called 'New Directions for Health'. The pre-publicity listed twenty-four distinguished speakers, professors of medicine, representatives of the World Health Organization, media specialists; an impressive array of expert speakers in nutrition, or high energy physics or child psychiatry (to pick a few blockbuster subjects at random).

The seminar sponsor was Blue Band margarine, who used it to promote their 'programme for positive health'.

The speakers did not mention the margarine. Yet Blue Band was around as background decoration, for it is important that there should be a connection made between a concept and an object — between health and a particular food. I will go so far as to say that the whole point of this seminar was to fuse concept and object so that, in the mind of the consumer in the supermarket, health means Blue Band margarine.

One hardly dares guess what it cost Blue Band to fly those distinguished speakers to Britain from all over the world. I would far prefer to see the money spent instead on a campaign for government legislation to have all food labelled adequately, so that we know what we are buying and eating.

20

Among margarines on the market, Blue Band is nowhere near the highest in polyunsatured fats. These are the fats which the consensus of medical opinion considers do no harm and might possibly be beneficial, while the mono-satured are neutral and the saturated fats are the villains. Imagine trying to suck up custard through a straw and you will have a suitably disgusting visual image of what the arteries have to do on a high-fat diet.

Blue Band margarine contains approximately 25 per cent polyunsaturated fats and 33 per cent saturated. Flora, which has had a health image for some years now, is high in polyunsaturated fats — 55 per cent and only 19 per cent saturated. And then there is Sainsbury's soya margarine which is as low as 12 per cent in saturated fats. Butter, by the way, is 63 per cent saturated and only 3 per cent polyunsaturated.

Van den Bergh, who own Blue Band, also own Flora and Krona, and are in turn owned by Unilever, who have 75 per cent of the margarine market. So Unilever sell the most saturated margarines (Krona is one, which is why it is supposed to taste like butter) and also the most poly-unsaturated margarines, and the same advertising company will often boost the sales, knowing that similar claims cannot be true of every variety of margarine.

Sound commercial business, no doubt, but the public is being left to flounder in a maze, often with signs pointing the wrong way.

Below are two tables with the information that the food companies are refusing to give you. Remember if a product simply says 'blended vegetable oils', it will be high in saturated fats, because it has almost certainly been made from palm or coconut oils. Many of the cheaper margarines are made from these oils. Olive oil is low in both polyunsaturated and saturated, but is very high in monosaturated fats, which are neutral. So olive oil is a far healthier cooking medium than butter.

Gold, which is what Weightwatchers recommend, is high in saturated fats, just over 40 per cent, and you might decide, now you know that butter is 63 per cent, to halve your consumption of butter and throw out the margarines. When we have the correct information we can decide for ourselves.

There is one school of thought that wishes the labels to show whether a fat is high, medium or low in poly-unsaturates, but this means that someone has to decide what percentages fall into these brackets. Margarines which now state 'high in polyunsaturates' mean 50 per cent polyunsaturates.

The low-fat spreads are neither margarines nor butter; they contain around 40 per cent fat, have a roughly equal mixture of saturated and polyunsaturated and the rest is mostly water. They are the most expensive water you can buy for your table.

I have not listed any so-called cooking fats, like Trex, Spar, Armour, as they are all very high in saturated fat. Any hard fat, like the one Mapletons make specifically for vegetarians called Nutter, will very likely be made from palm or coconut oil and therefore very high in saturated fats.

You will see from the tables below that each manufacturer is careful to provide a range of margarines which could fit into the brackets of high, medium and low in polyunsaturates. Unfortunately it is the cheaper brands of margarines which have a high saturated fat content. The message is, as always, if you are poor then you are expendable. You will be most at risk from coronary heart disease.

(It is important to remember that all figures are approximate. This is because the percentages tend to alter with each batch made.)

Vegetable Oils	Poly. %	Mono. %	Sat. %
Safflower oil	78.5	12.4	9.1
Sunflower oil	72.5	15.9	11.1
Kraft polyunsaturated oil	60.0	25.0	16.0
Tesco corn oil	59.0	27.0	13.0
Waitrose vegetable oil	59.0	25.0	15.0
Maize oil	56.6	28.3	14.3
Safeway corn oil	56.0	28.0	16.0
Mazola	52.0	33.0	15.0
Soya oil	52.0	24.6	15.4
Sesame oil	43.0	41.0	15.8
Peanut oil	32.5	43.1	17.6
Palm oil	9.1	44.1	46.8
Olive oil	8.5	74.0	16.0
Palm Kernel oil	2.0	15.5	82.5

Margarines			
Sainsbury Soya	55.0	25.0	12.0
Flora	54.0	24.0	19.0
Safeway Diet	53.0	24.0	10.0
Kraft Polyunsaturate Soft	48.8	26.0	24.0
Marks & Spencer Soft	48.0	31.0	21.0
Co-op Good Life	48.0	25.0	24.0
Tesco Super Soft	34.0	33.0	34.0
Safeway Pure Vegetable	30.0	51.0	19.0
Blue Band	25.0	40.0	33.0
Co-op Soft Silver	24.0	41.0	35.0
Safeway Table Soft	20.0	46.0	34.0
Tesco Table	15.0	27.0	58.0
Krona	11.0	45.0	44.0
Stork	8.0	47.0	41.0

The new vegetarian

The vegetarian movement in Britain has tended to give its cooking an unworthy image. I am referring to the nut loaf/cutlet syndrome. You will not find a recipe for either in this book. The reason behind it is understandable: the anxiety about protein. But the image has stuck and it will take some time to fade. It is an image of bland and stodgy cooking, hard pastry, sticky brown rice, nuts, beans and lentils. Cooking that deadens the palate and erupts in the gut.

To ensure that your own cooking does not err towards bland stodge, begin by studying every great classical cookery book for their sections on vegetables. Use the traditions of the best cuisines in the world to create the most delicate and seductive of vegetable dishes. The subcontinent of India has the most subtle of vegetable curries. (Never use packet curry powder: make your own; see Spices, pages 33-40). Explore the cuisines of the Far East where populations have lived for centuries on little or no meat at all.

Remove yourself from the strait-jacket concept of meals being three courses, with the main course having to be a meat substitute and two vegetables. There lies the path to mediocre cooking. And there was the mistake of the vegetarian movement in trying to ape the kind of meal meat-eaters were consuming.

Stop worrying about protein. We eat far too much protein in the Western industrialized societies. The protein we eat is more than twice what we need. There are, of course, in vegetarian fare, foods which are high in protein, the soybean and all the natural soy products (see Soybeans and derivatives, pages 43-59), but all pulses are high in protein.

Stop worrying about vitamins. A vegetarian diet especially needs no vitamin supplements. Vitamins B12, once thought to be lacking in plants, has now been discovered in all sea vegetables and in miso, a soy paste. A vegetarian diet is richer in vitamins and minerals than any other diet.

In the past the majority of people in Britain rarely ate meat, as they could not afford to. So there is no need to negate our own traditions. Laver bread, bubble and squeak, oatcakes, green pea soup, Sally Lunns, watercress cream soup, elderflower sorbet, fried sliced puffball, pease pudding and roast parsnips. All these and many more can be found in Susan Campbell's *English Cookery New and Old* (Hodder and Stoughton). Yet English vegetable recipes have almost to be dug out of the folk memory, because our reputation in the past has always been of vast consumption of meats and fowl. You would think that as an island nation which has far richer soil than any other European country, our traditions in food would be those of fish and vegetable. However, we do now grow a greater range of vegetables then ever before. I do not think it true that the British are slow to change and tend to be conservative, for we grow courgettes, peppers, aubergines, marmande tomatoes and mange-tout. But will the French grow runner beans?

Once you omit meat from the diet, you become increasingly aware of all the variety of vegetables on the market. You tend to experiment in cooking. Your imagination is put to the test. If you have your own garden, or a piece of land where you can grow your own vegetables, then consider yourself the most fortunate of beings. For you can then start to grow all the plants and vegetables which are commercially unobtainable or rare (see also Herbs, pages 31-33). Sorrel, Good King Henry, rocket, shallots, celeriac, Swiss chard, purslane, asparagus, chicory, radichio, lamb's lettuce, seakale, kohlrabi. Your own globe artichoke or corn-on-the-cob, picked half an hour before eating it, is a revelation of flavour compared with any which has lain on a stall in a market.

Remember, the longer the vegetables remain uncooked after picking, the more they lose their nutrients. An old potato has very little vitamin C content left in it. Try always to eat vegetables as fresh as possible. Vegetables which are limp or have frayed yellowing leaves might just as well be thrown on the compost heap.

The flat dweller can, with ingenuity, grow a few basic herbs in a window box, can keep a flourishing basil plant on a sunny window throughout the summer; can sprout seeds, alfalfa and mung beans, and so enjoy the freshness of foods grown for the pleasures of the table.

Try to eat salad once a day, either as a whole meal or part of a meal. Learn to bake your own bread; a low-calorie, high-protein loaf which uses soya flour (see pages 58 and 65) should be a staple part of your diet. Bread can be flavoured with herbs and seeds. A good bread is so satisfying that there is no need to spread it with butter or jam. Bread alone is not fattening.

Use more grains in your diet. Brown rice has long been a staple food for macrobiotics and in the wholefood cult, but there are other grains which now can be purchased from wholefood shops. Millet, cracked wheat (or burghul or bulgar wheat), spelt, oats, barley, rye. All these have a distinct flavour of their own. Often dry roasted, then boiled or steamed, they can be enjoyed with a few chopped fresh herbs or a little spring onion sprinkled over them.

When becoming vegetarian, the first essential is radically to change your store cupboard. This is much helped if you are not too far from a wholefood store; if they do not stock what you want, ask them to get it for you. If you have no wholefood store you will either have to use the mail order (Sunwheel Food's address is on page 60) or make do with a combination of the corner shop, the supermarket and the delicatessen. Large supermarkets are becoming more enterprising. They will respond to the consumer's opinion if it is voiced by a group, and is strong enough. If there is a public demand for foods unadulterated by additives and chemicals, foods which have not been over-refined and processed with their natural nutrition taken away, in the end the supermarkets and food manufacturers must bow to public opinion. (The National Housewives Association, 22 Great Pulteney Street, London W1, works in this field.)

A good wholefood shop will stock natural soy sauces, unrefined oils, rice vinegars, sea vegetables, Japanese pastas, dried mushrooms and tofu, as well as obscure and delicious condiments from the Far East. These could revolutionize your cooking. Certainly they will provide the opportunity to cook new dishes with flavours that seduce the palate. However, they are not necessary to eating well, though wonderfully welcome to have in the store cupboard on lazy days.

CHANGING OVER

The next section is for those meat-eaters who would like to try a vegetarian diet, but aren't quite sure where to begin. Shopping habits go hand-in-hand with menu-making — here, then, is a shopping list which will set you on the right lines, and menus for a whole week (lunch and dinner) which can be made from what you buy. All the recipes are given later in the book.

SHOPPING LIST

1 litre extra virgin olive oil	Packet of Hungarian paprika
1 litre sunflower oil	Bottle of gherkins
1 packet butter	8 oz sesame seeds
1 bottle toasted sesame oil	8 oz dried walnuts
1 dry cider vinegar	1 tiny packet of saffron
1 bottle dry sherry	1 bottle soy sauce
3 lb strong white bread flour	1 lb macaroni
3 lb wholemeal flour	Sea Salt

1 lb soy flour
1 lb plain white flour
1 large tin cornflour
1 packet frozen puff pastry
1 tin dried yeast
3 pints skimmed milk
1 tin skimmed milk powder
1 large carton yoghurt
1 large carton cottage cheese
1 large carton curd cheese
10 oz fromage frais or
  Quark
2 dozen eggs
1 packet Morinaga tofu
½ pint single cream
1 carton sour cream
1 lb mozzarella
1 lb sage Derby
1 lb fresh parmesan for
  grating
1 lb double Gloucester
½ lb gruyere
½ lb Roquefort
3 lb haricot beans
3 lb chick peas
3 lb bulgar wheat
3 lb rice
3 lb flageolet beans
1 packet wholemeal lasagne
Carton dried oregano
Carton dried marjoram

Bottle of capers
Black peppercorns
1 14oz tin of tomatoes
1 small tin tomato puree
8 oz black olives
3 lb onions
2 heads of celery
3 lb leeks
3 lb potatoes
2 lb mushrooms
6 lb tomatoes
6 heads of garlic
6 lemons
3 bunches spring onions
3 bunches each parsley and mint
2 cos lettuces or Webbs wonders
4 lb spinach
1 lb mange-tout peas
2 lb courgettes
1 broccoli
2 aubergines
5 oz ginger root
½ large pumpkin
3 avocados
8 ozs shallots
1 large cauliflower
6 green peppers
1 large cucumber
Extra vegetables for crudités:
Fennel/endive/celeriac/
  radishes

	Lunch	Dinner
Monday	Zuppa di Fagioli	Oeufs mollet with caper sauce Poireaux en croûte with grilled mushrooms
Tuesday	Tabbouleh and green salad	Hummus with crudités Pizza
Wednesday	Fried Sandwich	Tomato Soup Chinese stir-fried vegetables and boiled rice
Thursday	Macaroni Spinach	Pumpkin Soup Avocado flan & Salad
Friday	Pipérade	Mushroom Soup Galette de Chou Fleur
Saturday	Sesame Aubergine purée Flageolet purée Home-baked-whole-meal bread	Garlic Soup with saffron and potatoes Pancakes stuffed with egg and walnut
Sunday	Roquefort quiche	Stuffed cucumbers Lasagne Verde

Fresh fruits and cheeses to conclude dinner.

I give recipes for all the dishes in this week's menu (see Index).

STORES

A selection of the following would make a good store cupboard:

Sea salt, black pepper corns, sesame salt (see page 53), sesame seeds, sunflower and linseeds.

Dried yeast.

A choice of wine vinegars, brown rice vinegar, cider vinegar and flavoured herb vinegars, a black bean vinegar.

29

A choice of oils: sesame oil, extra virgin olive oil, sunflower or soy oil, peanut, walnut or almond oil.

A choice of sea vegetables.

Spices: red chillies, cloves, cardamom, cinnamon, coriander, cumin, fenugreek, root ginger, mace, nutmeg, allspice, mustard seed, poppy seed, turmeric.

Dried herbs: bay, caraway, chervil, dill weed and seed, marjoram, oregano, rosemary, sage, tarragon, thyme. (I do not think dried chives, parsley or mint are worth bothering about.)

Flours: wholemeal flour, strong white bread flour, soya flour, cornflour.

Cereals: brown rice, millet, bulgar wheat, oats, barley.

Pulses: flageolet, haricot, butter beans, chick peas, split peas, lentils (orange and green), soybeans, mung beans, aduki beans.

Flavourings: mustard powder, wasabi (Japanese horse-radish powder, hotter than ours) nori condiment (a sea vegetable purée) shoyu or tamari (see page 157), tekka (miso and roasted vegetables), vecon.

Capers. Miso paste. Tofu and soya milk. Lemons. Tin of green peppercorns.

Dried mushrooms.

Home-made pickles and chutney.

(Personally I have never cared for the taste of yeast extracts, which is why they are not listed here nor appear in any recipes. They are a basic ingredient in most vegetarian cooking though.)

One could cook marvellously well from a store cupboard one-eighth of the above, and one could cook disastrously with a store cupboard double the size. I spent one year living in Greece and the only store cupboard were the herbs growing on the mountain. I cooked in a hotel which had a huge cellar crammed with stores. Stores do not produce the art of cooking. Often they are not used for weeks, and then the choice of flavouring might be so discreet that no diner can actually pin it down. Nevertheless, stores are reassuring to the cook and they make spontaneous hospitality a lot easier.

HERBS

Not long ago I planned a herb garden, determined to grow and experiment with some of the more obscure herbs used infrequently now but widely eaten in the past like Good King Henry (which is part of the spinach and sorrel family), melilot (the clover family), red bergamot, salad burnet, Jacob's ladder, purslane and a good fifty more, most of which are thriving and give endless pleasure with their aroma and colour.

It is in the spring that the herb garden gives, I believe, the most intense satisfaction, for there are two herbs which stoutly ignore the worst of winter, and though in those months they are somewhat bludgeoned and subdued, immediately the first breath from a few mild days descends, they begin to grow. They are angelica, a biennial, and woad, a perennial. Their leaves can be chopped into salads, even in March, when we most need those fresh green leaves. Lovage, another tall stately herb, appears later; it is pungent with its own distinctive smell and flavour.

But I must not be disloyal to parsley, another biennial, for that too in the worst snows, will throw up a few lacy stalks and almost beg to be picked. It is there throughout the year and the leaves are rich in vitamins and iron. I use it constantly in salads and sauces. If you have great clumps of the curled parsley, pieces of it can be deep fried, and strangely delicious it is too. A curled frond can be plunged into sunflower or soy oil for little more than a minute, so that it is crisp, left to drain on a paper towel, then served while it is still hot. The absurd practice of using it as a garnish and not eating it is an ignorant waste.

Fennel is a tall perennial, both bronze and green, which turns the herb garden into an aesthetic pleasure. We associate it mostly as the herb to be eaten with fish — the poor on fast days ate only the fennel as they could not afford the fish — but its anise flavour goes well in iced soups or chopped and sprinkled over steamed vegetables. The seeds can be kept and stored throughout the winter.

Russian comfrey can be lightly cooked and eaten as a leaf vegetable, though some might be put off by the slight mucilaginous quality it has. For this reason it was an age-old cure for intestinal disorders and the leaves were also used as poultices. Comfrey fritters are delicious.

There are varieties of marjoram and of thyme, there are many mints, there are, at my last count, seventy-eight different herbs, many of which are to make teas or are medicinal. Many I have not yet tried, others look too beautiful to be picked.

Growing herbs is an addiction. But they enrich the vegetarian cuisine in ways that cannot be imagined. I have not mentioned rosemary or tarragon, herbs which again people associate only with lamb or fish, but a great sprig of rosemary cooked with haricot beans in a pressure cooker will flavour them nicely. French tarragon (avoid Russian tarragon like the plague, for it has no flavour and it spreads itself with pernicious abandon in the garden — unfortunately nurseries are somewhat remiss often selling their plants only as tarragon) can be cooked with courgettes or used as part of a stuffing for young vegetable marrows.

I have not mentioned basil. For that is not part of the herb garden. It is a tender annual and will not usually grow out of doors in Britain. But if the plants get enough sun and water they will flourish. Sow the seeds from March to Mid-April either in a greenhouse or on a sunny window sill. Plant them in pots and keep them well watered. I manage to get about one hundred plants from one packet of seeds. Through the summer I harvest the basil leaves and what I do not eat or make into pesto, I chop and mix with olive oil and freeze it for the winter. Basil is the classic herb to eat with tomatoes; it is one of the most fragrant herbs and its disciples are the most fervent and numerous.

Sadly, I have never been able to grow garlic. The cloves

seem to vanish once buried in the soil. In this book it is probably the most common ingredient. I have always felt passionate about its heady aroma and powerful flavour. But I am happy to say that not only would all my culinary skills be depleted if garlic did not exist, but also my diet would lack an important health giving property. For garlic reduces the chances of coronary heart disease. Its anti-septic substances calm the digestive system and help to clear bronchitis. It is the Emperor of all flavourings.

SPICES

We tend to think of spices as related just to curries and of the spices for a curry as coming out of a packet or jar. If we can get rid of both fallacies, then a whole, new, expanding range of dishes opens before us. Or let me put it another way: there are hundreds of dishes, including many permutations of spices, which we would not think of as curries. That is because comercial brands of curry powder use a standard mixture of spices which have convinced us that that is the true flavour. I would find it gratifying if everyone threw their packets of curry powder into the bin and we all began to create our own.

In India there are many hundreds of different flavours, which all basically derive from about twenty-four ingre-dients. Given even half that number, we could mix our own curry pastes for the rest of our lives and never, but never, come up with a mixture that resembles the taste from a packet.

Remember that the hotness of the curry comes mainly from chillies, either ground into a powder, or dried — these are the tiny red chillies — or from fresh green chillies. These can be kept separate from your main mixture, so that you can regulate how hot you want your curry to be. Three or four tiny dried red chillies will enflame a large casserole of vegetables, as will two teaspoons of chilli powder, as will four green chillies chopped up with the rest of the vegetables. So being able to create a really hot curry is never a problem.

Cayenne pepper and ginger will also give you a degree of hotness. While appreciating the flavour of grated root ginger, I don't much care for the flavour of powdered ginger — though we tend to associate it with Chinese cooking more than Indian. Cayenne pepper is a fiery element and one I would be circumspect about.

Turmeric is the spice which turns curries the colour of yellow ochre, it is also the flavour which asserts itself in all commerical brands of curry powder. You can choose to use it or not.

Other spices are: black pepper, cloves, cinnamon, cardamom, coriander, cumin, curry leaves (see below), fenugreek, mace, nutmeg or allspice, mustard and poppy seed.

All spices are at their best when fresh; it is worth buying them at an Indian store and having containers which keep out the light as well as the air. The spices should be roasted before they are ground and, as they all need different times and care must be taken to ensure they do not brown, they have to be roasted separately. However, it is not a long or tedious job, for each spice roasted in an open saucepan will exude its basic aroma within a minute or soon after. Hold the pan over a high heat and shake it so that the spices do not stick; they will change colour slightly as they exude their oil. They will also now be easier to grind. Do this using a coffee grinder, and keep the powder in an air-tight jar.

You need not use all of the above spices. You could, for example, make a powder out of the first six. Indeed using those spices, you could mix them in different ratios and you would have a dozen different flavours. Tom Stobart in his book *Herbs, Spices and Flavourings* (Penguin) gives a table showing some of the many permutations. It is up to the individual cook to experiment, tasting each mixture and discovering your favourites.

Many recipes for making your own curry powder also

include garam masala, which is odd, because that too is a mixture of spices, all of them used in curry powder. But in India garam masala is not used as curry powder. Instead it is usually added at the end of cooking, or sprinkled — as we use salt and pepper — over the meal when it is served. Basically the masala is black pepper, coriander, cumin, cloves and cinnamon, roasted and finally ground. Commercial brands which can be bought at Indian stores also have ginger, pimento, bay leaves and nutmeg in them. There are many dishes which would be flavoured with just garam masala and no other spices.

The ground spices always have to be fried first in oil or ghee before you add the vegetables and continue the cooking. Using a curry paste avoids the initial frying, and for some dishes (for instance, when the spices are mixed with yoghurt and the vegetable is marinated in the mixture) a paste is much easier to use. Because the spices are in a liquid suspension their flavour matures. So remember that the older a paste is the more violent in flavour and hotness it is liable to be. It might have medium curry on the label, but a whiff of it is likely to unblock the sinuses forever! Curry pastes are not difficult to make and it is satisfying to use your own mixtures.

Vindaloo Paste
25 g/1 oz dried red chillies
275 ml/½ pint wine vinegar
2 heads of garlic
50 g/2 oz root ginger
1 teaspoon each of roasted cumin, mustard seed, coriander seed, and mace.
275 ml/½ pint vegetable oil
2 teaspoons salt

Soak the red chillies in the vinegar for a day. Peel the garlic and the ginger, chop finely. Pop the chilli vinegar, garlic and ginger into a blender and liquidize. Meanwhile grind all the roasted spices into a powder.

Put the oil into a pan and add the spices, cook for about 10 minutes, or until the spices (which will become a paste) have begun to separate from the oil. Add the vinegar mixture and the salt slowly, stir well. Leave to cool, then bottle.

You sometimes find a bunch of 'curry leaves' in Indian stores. It is worth purchasing them if they smell fairly strongly of curry. If you add a few to the ghee or oil with a teaspoon of ground coriander and mustard seed, you will have an authentic and unique flavour. These leaves are to the sub-continent what coriander leaves are to the Middle East and what garlic is to a French market. The smell permeates the houses and the air you breathe.

Ghee is clarified butter. Most recipes use it for the initial frying, as butter is inclined to burn because of the tiny percentage of milk solids and sugar. These are eliminated when you strain melted butter through muslin. Our butter when clarified does not have the same flavour as Indian ghee. You can buy ghee in tins (it will keep in the refrigerator for many months after being opened) or you can start the cooking with a flavourless vegetable oil. For the best results, though, ghee is essential. Because of the way it is made it has a particular flavour and as long as the food is not drowned in a muliplicity of spices, one can taste it. (Ghee contains a high proportion of saturated fats. If you are being circumspect on your intake of fat, then use a vegetable oil which is high in polyunsaturated fat: sunflower, soya, maize; see Fats, page 23.)

It might well be a golden rule for Europeans to remember that Indian cooking at its best is subtle. It is a careful blending of a few particular spices which have been chosen to enhance a particular vegetable. The Indian sub-continent has, after all, the longest and richest tradition of vegetarian cooking in the world.

There is something distinctly pretentious about me, Anglo-Saxon to the core, writing about curries. And I pretend to no great knowledge of them. But I have used spices in cooking for half a lifetime and many of those dishes have been curries, and it must have been in the swinging Sixties when, in a moment of anarchy, I threw the commercial curry powders into the dustbin. So the recipes I give are a very few of the great many that I have enjoyed making. I have purposely chosen those which do not strike us immediately as curries — I mean that you will not find here the vegetables immersed in great bowls of steaming brown aromatic soup. Nothing wrong with that; but this is what we Europeans tend to think of as 'curry' and is also quite often what we eat in Indian restaurants, for many excellent restaurants merely cook what they think we want to eat.

After the initial expenditure on the spices, curries must be one of the most economical of dishes, even in the vegetarian repertoire. And the range of vegetable curries is enormous. Consider: there are dhals, lentil purées made from black peas, yellow or green lentils, split or whole, flavoured with spices. There are the koftas, purées of vegetable dried, mixed with spices, rolled into golf-ball shapes and fried. There are tarkaris, where the vegetables are fried with spices, and the heat is raised at the last minute so that the curry is dry and almost crisp.

There are yoghurt salads and stuffed cabbages, peppers, tomatoes and marrows, stuffed not with rice, but with ginger, chillies, and spices. There are all the curd dishes, where the vegetables are cooked in a spiced yoghurt paste, as in the baked spiced potatoes below. There are the stuffed puris (dough enclosing vegetables and spices), the samosas (a pastry made from flour and ghee) or the pakoras (spiced batters).

The only way to begin to understand such richness is to be fortunate enough to have Indian friends whose knowledge and talents you can tap. Lock them in the kitchen and learn, learn, learn.

Baked Spiced Potatoes

4 large potatoes
275 ml/$\frac{1}{2}$ pint yoghurt
4 crushed bay leaves
1 teaspoon each turmeric, coriander, and chilli powder
50 g/2 oz ghee
1 tablespoon honey
4 crushed cloves garlic
1 teaspoon salt
Handful of chopped coriander leaves

You first make a yoghurt paste to marinate and cook the potatoes in. Fry the bay leaves and the rest of the spices in the ghee for a few minutes, add the yoghurt, honey and salt. Mix well.

Peel the potatoes and boil them whole for about 12 minutes, so that the outside is soft. Prick them all over with a fork and roll them in the yoghurt paste. Leave for an hour, turning the potatoes once or twice. Use a shallow fireproof dish which you can then put into the preheated oven at 400°F/200°C/Gas Mark 6 for about 30 minutes. Sprinkle with the coriander leaves before serving.

Fried Carrots in Yoghurt

675 g/1$\frac{1}{2}$ lb carrots
50 g/2 oz ghee
50 g/2 oz ginger root
6 cloves garlic
2 teaspoons each of sesame and poppy seeds
1 teaspoon each of turmeric, cumin, coriander, and chilli powder
14 ml/5 oz carton yoghurt
Handful of chopped coriander leaves
1 teaspoon salt

Grate ginger root and chop garlic. Peel and slice carrots thinly. Choose a large saucepan so that you can stir and turn the carrots as they will cook without water. Melt the ghee in the pan, add carrots and salt, let them cook for a moment until the steam begins to rise. Stir and turn them with a wooden spoon, while you add all of the spices, ginger and garlic. Let it cook a few minutes more, then add the yoghurt, stir and put the lid back on to the saucepan. Let it simmer until the carrots are cooked through, about 15 minutes. Sprinkle with the coriander leaves before serving.

Cauliflower Curry
1 large cauliflower
6 crushed cloves of garlic
50 g/2 oz ginger root
1 teaspoon each paprika, turmeric, and garam masala
Juice from 1 lemon
25 g/1 oz ghee or 2 tablespoons vegetable oil

Cut cauliflower into smallish chunks. Peel and grate ginger root. Heat the oil or ghee, fry the ginger, crushed garlic, paprika and turmeric for a minute, then add the lemon juice and the cauliflower. Place lid on saucepan and let it simmer for about 4 to 5 minutes. The cauliflower should still be slightly firm. Sprinkle with the garam masala and serve.

Grated Cabbage with Ginger
1 medium white cabbage
50 g/2 oz ginger root
1 teaspoon coriander powder
25 g/1 oz ghee or 2 tablespoons vegetable oil
1 teaspoon salt
1 teaspoon garam masala
1 tablespoon coconut

Peel and grate the ginger root. Melt the ghee or oil, add the ginger and coriander powder, and cook for a moment or two. Meanwhile grate the whole of the cabbage and add it to the oil and spices, raise the flame and stir so that the pieces of cabbage are sealed by the oil or ghee. Cook so that it heats through and the steam is rising, then add the salt.

Take away from the flame immediately and serve with the garam masala and the coconut sprinkled over it.
    The cabbage is hardly cooked at all and tastes all the better for it.

Spiced Onion Salad
3 onions
1 green chilli
Tablespoon chopped coriander leaves
1 teaspoon salt
2 tablespoons wine vinegar
140 ml/5 oz carton yoghurt

Slice onions thinly, sprinkle them with salt and let them marinate in the wine vinegar for about an hour. Chop the green chilli as finely as you can — this will make the salad very hot, so you may wish to omit it. Drain the onion, mix the coriander leaves, chilli and onion with the yoghurt. Allow to stand for a further hour before serving.

CHILDREN AND A MEATLESS DIET

We all know there is a practical alternative to feeding the kids with fish fingers or bangers and mash, but can we be bothered to explore it? How much time and trouble will it cost us and is it worth it when quite obviously the kids themselves prefer the convenience foods and they are going to refuse to eat anything else anyway? What about television advertising, school meals, and their best friend's mother who has never eaten anything except out of a tin?
    I often receive letters from anxious mums with vege-tarian children, asking whether the diet contains enough protein. For them, and for others, I explain in detail on

pages 43-59 how to use the soybean, that miracle food; how we can benefit from tofu, a Chinese bean curd, and Japanese miso, a fermented bean paste and their byproduct, soy sauce; and also from the soya flour, grits, flakes and textured vegetable protein that we manufacture in the West.

On average, soybeans have thirty-three per cent more protein than any other crop. They contain the eight essential amino acids, the sources of complete protein. On a weight-by-weight comparison, soya has twice the protein of meat, four times that of eggs and seventeen times that of milk.

We should also consider that from the moment of their birth we are training our children in habits of eating which directly affect their health. For example, the build-up of coronary disease begins in childhood. More than twenty other diseases common to Western man (including dental decay, which is the only one you hear about) can be prevented by a healthy and sensible diet. For these reasons we should bother, and we should not care how much time and trouble it costs us.

But there is just not enough information available on what is healthy and what is not. What there is, is sometimes downright conflicting and there are always conflicting opinions which exploit our confusion.

Take the daily pinta. No harm in the kids knocking that back? Alas, we have been misled. In the United Kingdom we are encouraged to drink full-fat milk, and that is the biggest single source of saturated fat in our diet. The government gives a subsidy to local authorities as a contribution to free school milk, but the subsidy is specifically for full-fat milk and not for skimmed. The aim of the subsidy is to reduce the fall in milk sales, because farmers get more money from liquid milk than by manufacturing cheese or butter. Thus the Ministry of Agriculture benefits farmers at the possible expense of our schoolchildren's health.

The important nutrients in milk are all found in the skim

— the protein, calcium and riboflavin. The fat contains vitamin A and D, but an ordinary diet will contain those anyway. If we want to avoid the beginning of coronary diseases in our children and begin to lay down good eating habits, then we should drink skimmed milk only. The government does not wish to encourage us to drink more skimmed milk, or to use the EEC subsidy which applies also to skimmed or semi-skimmed milk, because the surplus butter-fat will accumulate in the butter mountain. Local authorities should provide skimmed milk for schools and put pressure upon the government to give them a subsidy to do so. It is heartening that more and more large self-service stores now stock liquid skimmed milk.

Another vital eating habit to obliterate in the home is the sugar bowl, which should not be on the table or even in the larder. Children acquire a taste for sweetness. The manufacturers of baby foods have been asked not to put added sugar into their products.

We should also take note of how much salt we are using and try to appreciate food without it. Too much fat, sugar and salt are all the food habits we have grown up with and which we continue to give our children unless we can change them now.

The Vegetarian Baby by Sharon Yntema (Thorsons Publishers) is comprehensive on the subject. It includes a look at babies in other cultures, analyses our nutritional requirements, and talks about the attitude of meat-eating grandparents (who tend to fuss over their vegetarian grandchildren, certain that parents are depriving them). It goes into pregnancy and diet, lactation and diet, weaning and the vegetarian working parent. There is a large section on food preparation and a small collection of recipes for babies. There is no section for children older than fourteen months because by then they are eating more or less what we are eating ourselves.

If you are going to drop convenience foods, you need to prepare yourself, the kitchen and the store cupboard. Start in a modest way by keeping two days out of the week for home-made meals. Do your reading beforehand. The Vegetarian Centre and Bookship at 58 Marloes Road, London W8 6LA, will help by suggesting books on how to become vegetarian, on health and nutrition for children and adults. There are also local vegetarian branches all over the United Kingdom.

Learn to make your own bread. It is not just wholemeal which is delicious, but home-made white, granary, rye, or barley bread are all a revelation. A few slices from such a loaf with soup is the best winter lunch in the world.

I am astonished at how many tins of soup fill up the trolleys in supermarkets when home-made soup is so cheap and delicious. I estimate that in a family of four, dropping convenience foods altogether would save up to £12 per week.

SOYBEANS AND DERIVATIVES

It is ironic that the soybean with its protein richness is the dullest of all the dried peas and beans. It has been dismissed by gourmets and all distinguished cookery writers. One can understand why, for there are few recipes in books devoted to the bean which sound even vaguely appetising. It should not be beyond the wit of an enterprising cook to create a dish which is delicious and nutritious — yet I confess it has strained the wit of *this* enterprising cook.

The beans were first grown in Kew at the end of the eighteenth century. There are over a thousand varieties of soy — which is not a bean at all; it belongs to the pea family — and in such a range, there ought to be one or two that are delicious. The problem is finding them.

The soybean stocked in wholefood shops is the round beige-coloured one, and possibly the small black bean. There is little difference in taste between the two. Both varieties need soaking for around ten hours in cold water, though if you pour boiling water over the beans, they need little more than an hour. A bean is soaked completely if it will split into two and the insides are flat and not concave. If soaked for too long, goodness is lost in the water. Drain the soaking water from the beans and use new water for the cooking.

Another irony is that the soybean, unlike other pulses, has a substance called 'trypsin inhibitor' which blocks a trypsin enzyme essential for the digestion of protein. The key is for them to be thoroughly cooked, then the trypsin inhibitor is destroyed. If simmered on top of the stove, soybeans will need around four to five hours. One of the best methods is to cook them overnight in a solid fuel burner, or in an electric casserole. They can also be pressure-cooked for twenty-five minutes.

This is the science, but so far we are nowhere near the art. The main problem is that if the bean is left whole while cooking it refuses with steadfast obstinacy to soak up any flavours around it. Hence, you have the insulated bland bean sitting amidst a sea of sauce. Breaking up the bean at the end of cooking helps. One whirl in the liquidizer will crush the bean into several bits, or a little hard work with the potato masher will do the trick too. Yet the bean bits still taste of nothing very much.

When the beans are pulped — blend the beans for a couple of moments until you have a thick grainy purée — they can, at last, be flavoured. The beans can also be pulped after soaking, and the pulp cooked, when the cooking times ought to be half that for the whole beans.

The cooked pulp can be mixed with chopped vegetables, and spoonsful of this mixture can be rolled in breadcrumbs, sesame, poppy or mustard seeds, and then fried. If the mixture is too liquid a tablespoon of soya flour will thicken it, or if it needs binding, add a beaten egg. I would tend to use strong flavourings — shallots, onions, garlic and herbs.

Served with a miso sauce, these soybeans croquettes can be far more delicious than they sound.

In America you can buy packets of dry roasted soybeans, salted like peanuts. While the nuts have 27 per cent protein, the beans have 20 per cent more. Packets come in plain, salted, garlic or barbecue flavour.

You can roast your own at home. Using an oiled baking tray, spread the soaked, drained beans over the tray and place in a pre-heated oven 350°F/180°C/Gas Mark 4 for about 2½ hours, or until they are golden dark and crisp. Shake them twice, at the end of each hour. Toss the roasted beans in a flavoured salt, celery, garlic or sesame, or in your own flavouring made out of herbs and spices.

If the roasted beans are left unsalted you can make 'kinako'. Grind the roasted beans, or blend them in a liquidizer, until they are a powder. This flour has no gluten so it will not thicken, but it can be used to coat food before frying. It can also be mixed with butter or margarine, miso or ground peanut or sesame, to make a paste for toast and biscuits. In Japan they sweeten kinako and use it to coat confectionery. It must be the only example of chewy sweets which could be good for you.

The recipes here are for the whole bean, an attempt at solving the challenge of their insipid flavour. The first recipe is an alternative to roasting the beans.

Sesame soybeans

100 g/7 oz soybeans
Sunflower oil
Tablespoon sesame salt (that is 1 of sea salt to 5 of roasted ground sesame; see page 53).

Soak the beans, drain them, lay them out to dry on paper towels. Have 1 cm/½ in of sunflower oil in a deep pan, throw in the beans, fry them for about 10 to 12 minutes. They are done when medium brown and crisp. Let them drain on absorbent paper and, when cool mix in sesame salt. They will keep for months, if they are in an airtight container.

Soybean Russian salad

100 g/3½ oz each of baby carrots, fresh peas, broad beans, French beans, celery
2 small green peppers, chopped
200 g/7 oz cooked soybeans
chopped parsley or mint

For the Mayonnaise

2 egg yolks
1 teaspoon mustard powder
2 cloves garlic, crushed
275 ml/½ pint sunflower oil

Cook the baby carrots, fresh peas, broad and French beans. Dice carrots and beans into four. Add diced raw celery and green peppers, then cooked soybeans. Make a mayonnaise with the egg yolks, mustard powder, crushed cloves of garlic and sunflower oil. Toss the vegetables and soybeans in the mayonnaise and add before serving a sprinkling of chopped parsley or mint.

Soybean fritters

200 g/7 oz soybeans, cooked
200 g/7 oz brown rice, cooked
4 small onions, chopped
2 cloves garlic, crushed
1 teaspoon each of ground rosemary, dill seed, marjoram, celery salt
Pinch of cayenne pepper or chilli powder
1 egg
1½ tablespoons soya flour
sunflower oil
sesame oil

Mix the ingredients well together. Fry spoonfuls of this mixture in sunflower oil which has been flavoured with a few drops of sesame oil. Fry until crisp on both sides.

Black soybean casserole

200 g/7 oz black beans
2 tablespoons olive oil
large piece of ginger root
6 cloves of garlic, crushed
water or stock
1 tablespoon miso

Soak the black beans. In the olive oil, fry a golf-ball size piece of ginger root, grated, and the crushed cloves of garlic for a moment to flavour the oil. Then add the beans and fry those for a few more moments. Add enough water or stock to cover the top of the beans by about an inch. Cook them as described on pages 43-44. When the beans are soft, add the liquid to the miso, mix well together and pour back into the casserole.

Miso

Miso, sometimes referred to as fermented soybean paste, is made from soybeans, cereals or rice, salt, water and a culture. It is a living food like yoghurt. It was brought to Japan from China, about two and a half thousand years ago.

Over the centuries the Japanese have made miso into a distinctive cult of their own cuisine. Home-made miso is brewed at small farms and large Buddhist monasteries, and carries its year of origin and district. Connoiseurs of miso can roll a little on the tongue, wax lyrical on its individual qualities, and then tell you its location.

In the early Sixties, when the macrobiotic movement took up miso as an essential part of its diet, Japan began to export large quantities to the United States. Much of the miso we now buy in the West is made in factories, which speed up the fermentation time. This fermentation is the key to the high nutritional value of miso: it breaks down the soybean into digestible amino acids. As with cheese and yoghurt, it is the added culture and the time it takes to work which imparts the distinctive aroma and flavour.

The Book of Miso by William Shurtleff and Akiko Aoyago (Autumn Press Inc.) is the definitive work on the subject. The authors claim that miso is a protein booster, aids digestion, should be used instead of salt in a low salt diet, and is essential in low-fat cookery because it is free of cholesterol. The book contains four hundred recipes, too American for my own taste, but an excellent source of ideas.

Some of the health-giving properties which they claim for miso — that it helps to develop a strong resistance to disease, for instance — have as yet little scientific backing. Yet the most incredible claim of all — that miso can prevent radiation sickness — has been substantiated. Perhaps the government should look into the research done by Japanese scientists on the way miso can expel radioactive strontium from the body. Sixty million kegs imported now from Japan and distributed free to the nation would be of more practical use than a pamphlet.

In Japan you can buy over a hundred different varieties of miso. In New York I counted fifteen different types. Here, you can choose between only two or three, but they are perfect for an introduction. They can be bought in 450 g/1 lb packs amazingly economically, considering that two and a half teaspoons of miso will give you all of your protein requirements for a day.

'Mugi' miso is made from soybeans and barley, while 'genmai' is made from soybeans and brown rice. My own favourite is 'hatcho', which has a higher proportion of beans in it and therefore more protein. But it is by far the most strongly flavoured. I suspect newcomers to miso will find that both mugi and genmai are strong enough.

When I first bought miso, over ten years ago, I was both ignorant and vague. I thought of it as a substitute for meat stock in soups. I used it in the winter to flavour vegetables and bean soups, but I made a great mistake — I cooked it. I added the miso with the raw vegetables and while it all simmered away I innocently thought it was imparting richness and flavour. It did the exact opposite. Cooking miso destroys the culture and all the flavour. In fact, those soups were rather nasty and that packet of miso was thrust to the back of the refrigerator and stayed there for years. Miso will keep for ages, in or out of the refrigerator. Sometimes a slight mould may begin, but that can be scraped off.

Miso can, in fact, be heated, but at most for a few minutes. As a general rule, think of miso as an addition which will enrich the food at the end of cooking.

Another mistake is to take out the packet of miso and spoon a dollop of it into the soup or casserole, stir, and think it will work. It won't — it will go lumpy. Miso needs an initial mixing before being added to other foods.

As miso is of such strong flavour, it is best to mix it gently with yoghurt, oil, tahini, vinegar, peanut butter, or just plain hot water, before adding to the dish itself. In this way you will have a smooth thin purée to be gently stirred in and the flavour will be dispersed. Never add salt to a dish where you will be adding miso.

The Japanese, like others in the East, place themselves into a serene state of mind before cooking, as the preparation and cooking of food is one facet of the creative philosphy of life. Miso is a food which refuses to be hurried. Whatever you do with it needs to be thought out and planned ahead. It demands respect and love — a difficult concept for our Western heritage, though the same philosophy permeates French cuisines. But probably miso is also a natural tranquilizer, so once it is part of your daily diet you will become serene anyway.

Miso spread (to be used on toast and biscuits)
1 packet miso
3 tablespoons water
3 tablespoons honey
100 g/4 oz walnuts, crushed

This can be made up to your own personal taste. Mix ingredients together in a pan, heat gently and stir.

When thoroughly amalgamated and smooth, pour into a jar. Refrigerated, it will keep for ever.

Instead of walnuts, you could add other nuts, or ground roasted sesame seeds or dried herbs. Instead of honey you could add peanut butter or tahini paste. Instead of water, you could add wine. The Japanese often use half water and half sake.

Miso vegetable soup

This can be made using any one vegetable, or a mixture of vegetables. Slice them thinly and sauté in sunflower oil for a few minutes. Because of the miso you do not need the richness of butter or olive oil. Add two quarts of water and simmer. When the vegetables are tender, add a cup of the soup to two tablespoons of miso in a bowl and stir well. Add the miso to the rest of the soup. Take from the heat and leave for five minutes with the lid on the saucepan.

Miso eggs with courgettes

3 courgettes
sunflower oil
1 tablespoon miso
3 tablespoons water
2 eggs
chopped fresh herbs

Slice the courgettes diagonally, about ½ cm/¼ inch thick and sauté in a little sunflower oil until just *al dente*. Have ready the tablespoon of miso mixed with the water and beaten eggs. Pour in the miso egg mixture and toss the courgettes in it, so that they are lightly covered in the cooked egg. Serve with a sprinkling of chopped fresh herbs.

Miso sauce for pasta

2 or 3 onions, thinly sliced
2 or 3 clovers of garlic, crushed

1 tablespoon sunflower oil
450 g / 1 lb tomatoes, steamed and sieved
1 tablespoon miso
Fresh basil, parsley or marjoram, chopped

Sauté the onions, and crushed cloves of garlic, in oil. When soft add the pulp from the tomatoes that have been steamed and sieved. Heat, then pour a little of the sauce into a bowl which contains miso. Mix well, return to pan and before serving add some chopped fresh basil, parsley or marjoram.

Tofu

There was a cartoon in the *New Yorker* of a wife serving a suckling pig, while her husband sourly remarks, 'Not tofu disguised again.' Tofu is a soybean curd and has been made in China for two millennia. Buddhist monks in the sixth century made elaborate representations of fish and poultry out of tofu. In the United States, thanks to the moral health movement, tofu has become an 'in' food.

Americans are six per cent of world population but consume thirty per cent of its meat and dairy products. The vegetarian minority — estimated at ten million — are blazingly articulate in their diatribes against this injustice. They have also had a tremendous impact on the food market in New York, where there are countless wholefood shops and restaurants, selling reasonably priced high quality food.

In Europe we are less sensitive. The EEC comes third — after Canada — in the consumption of meat and dairy products, but tofu is not likely to be a subject of a cartoon in *Punch*. Nor do we seem to be as aware of an alternative diet, healthier and less harmful to underdeveloped countries. Tofu is the key to such a diet. It is time we learnt about it.

Tofu has more protein, relative to calories, than any other food. It ought to be essential in all slimming diets; but in which one does it appear? Tofu has no cholesterol, is abundant in minerals and vitamins (some tofu can have as much as fifty per cent more calcium than dairy milk) and is probably the most versatile of foods. It can be eaten hot or cold, as an appetizer, or for any course in a main meal.

It is bland, the only subtle variety of flavour coming from the type of solidifier used to make the soybean purée curdle. But that also means it soaks up and adapts to a variety of flavours.

William Shurtleff and Akiko Aoyago have again written the definitive work, *The Book of Tofu* (Autumn Press Inc.) available at Cranks and all health stores which stock a range of publications.

Recipes exist for making tofu out of soy powder and soy flour. I cannot recommend those which I have tried. Both the powder and the flour have already been processed, losing a percentage of protein.

Theoretically, you could also make tofu out of soya milk, now manufactured by Granose Foods Limited, and marketed widely in whole food shops. Again, I cannot see the advantage, especially when the soya milk itself is so delicious and such a boon for vegans and children allergic to dairy milk. The last time I tasted soya milk as good as this was in Singapore where it is sold on street corners in iced cans, and it was bought with as much enthusiasm as we buy lager.

Up to now, those fortunate enough to be near a Chinese store have bought their home-made tofu there. It retails at a modest price for 450 g/1 lb, enough for six people. But now I am delighted to welcome a new tofu. Sunwheel Foods, whose products are always of impeccable quality, are marketing a tofu made by Morinaga and imported from Japan. It is more refined than the Chinese home product and slightly dearer. It can be bought in most health and whole food shops: if they do not yet stock it, insist that they begin. Because of its blandness it is perfect for babies and young children. It can be mixed with honey, fruit, grains and nuts, and could be used as a substitute for cream in a pudding.

However, it is the tofu recipes for adults that I find more stimulating. For many dishes, it is traditionally flavoured with shoyu or tamari, with varieties of miso and sesame pastes, or with grated ginger, hot radish and flavoured vinegars. As an hors d'oeuvres, chilled sliced tofu could be served with several sauces in shallow bowls, the tofu dipped into the sauce with chopsticks. Tofu can be beaten into a purée and used as a salad dressing. It can be mixed with cottage cheese, garlic, paprika and herbs, for a superior liptauer cheese.

But first drain your tofu well. Slide it out of the packet with care (the Morinaga tofu is less solidified than the Chinese) and on to paper towels, leave in the refrigerator for a good couple of hours, or better still, overnight. Then slice it into the size you want and drain the cut size again for another hour. If it is sliced at the start it will tend to crumble.

Both sesame oil and sesame salt are often used in tofu recipes. Sesame seeds are part of the diet in the East. They, too, are high in protein and low in polyunsaturates. Sesame oil can be bought in Chinese stores and wholefood shops. For me, it has become indispensable. A few drops will flavour a salad or the sunflower oil in stir-frying.

Sesame salt
Roast the sesame seeds, about 200 g/7 oz at a time, heating them in a closed saucepan over a moderate heat. Shake the pan all the time, until you hear the seeds popping. Keep shaking the pan for another two minutes, and then take it off the heat. If the seeds are dark golden brown they are done. Grind the seeds to a powder. Mix one part of sea salt to five parts of sesame powder. We now use it at the table instead of plain sea salt. Guests become addicted, rush home and start making their own. Make any amount you like, for it keeps happily in an airtight container.

Stir-fried tofu

1 packet tofu
Large piece of ginger root
3 large cloves of garlic, crushed
2 tablespoons sunflower oil
Handful of mange-touts
6 small onions, quartered
6 courgettes, sliced
2 tablespoons shoyu

Cut a well-drained packet of Morinaga tofu into 1 cm/½ inch slices. Grate a golf ball size piece of ginger root and crush the garlic into the oil. Heat the oil in a wok or frying pan, let the garlic and ginger cook for a moment, and then add a handful of mange-touts, the quartered onions and sliced courgettes. Fry for a few minutes stirring all the time. When the vegetables have just begun to soften and shrink a little, add the tofu. Fry for another two minutes. Take from the heat and add the shoyu. Serve with brown rice.

Sesame tofu

Slice the cubed tofu into 5 cm/2 inch squares, ½ cm/¼ inch thick. Dip them in roasted ground sesame. Coat the pieces like breadcrumbs. Fry in olive oil for a few minutes until brown and crisp.

Tofu salad dressing

1 packet tofu
2 tablespoons olive oil
1 teaspoon lemon juice or wine vinegar
3 tablespoons shoyu
Handful chopped parsley or mint

Blend all the ingredient together. You will have a thick creamy purée.

Tofu-stuffed pancakes

Use a well-flavoured batter. Mine was:

100 g/4 oz wholemeal flour
2 eggs
140 ml/¼ pint shoyu
140 ml/¼ pint water

Slice tofu into chip lengths, fry in one tablespoon of sunflower oil and one teaspoon of sesame oil, add two sliced courgettes and let them brown. Make the pancakes, stuff them with the tofu and courgettes and serve with a sauce made from fresh tomatoes.

TVP

There is now a large range of soybean products (all made with soya flour) on the shelves of your local health and wholefood shops. They can be roughly divided into three categories:

Textured vegetable protein or TVP which comes in packets of meat-flavoured chunks, 'cutlets' or granules.

Packets of TVP granules already mixed with herbs, spices, dried vegetables and a list of vitamins and additives as long as your arm.

Soya flour itself, soya flakes and soya grits.

The names are all gastronomically unappealing. Which of us wants our food textured? Grits remind one of a dusty road and as for the TVP mixtures, they have labels like 'sosmix' and 'burgermix' which do nothing to whet my appetite.

I am not a vegetarian who has ever missed meat, so I did not need to search for a substitute and I was not very sympathetic to the whole concept of TVP. You might say I was irritated even, for it is a bizarre irony that soybeans which ought to be feeding the under-nourished should be processed to resemble animal flesh for the vegetarian minority in the affluent West.

And if you have recently given up meat and feel its absence, I cannot think that a soya beef chunkie will fill the gap. No one could honestly say it bears any resemblance in

55

texture, and it has only the faintest in flavour. In the trade it is known as spun protein, and it costs more than the soya granules because it is more complicated to make. The protein, after being treated with alkalies, is spun through tiny holes, then stretched, bound and shaped. The ingenuity of man must be admired when you consider he can even make a 'chicken leg' or a strip of 'bacon' out of this substance. Until, that is, you stick your knife into it and discover it has the sad bounce of a punctured and very damp lilo.

I cannot think how one would use this quasi-meat in a palatable dish. I once curried it with vegetables but the soya pieces still behaved like shredded trampoline.

Most carnivores will have eaten TVP granules without knowing, for food manufacturers use them in pies, stews, curries and sausages. I once used some to make a sham shepherds pie, but the dish had little joy in it. (But this is a personal opinion. Many people find that TVP is a great boon as a convenience food in a busy life when they have principles about vegetarianism but do not feel all that strongly about the aesthetics of food.)

The manufactured rissole mixtures are useful standbys. You mix them with water, leave for a few minutes, then shape and fry. On the whole they taste better than one would think. There is a wide range of them, and some taste better than others. You can, of course, add extra herbs and onions if you wish. But if you sit down to, say, your 'burgermix' expecting to tuck into something akin to a hamburger, you will be disappointed. I enjoyed mine, but it is unlike anything else I've eaten. It did not resemble meat, nor minced beans and vegetables. It looked a little like toy stuffing and tasted like a mild stock cube. I laced it with shoyu sauce and a good quality mustard and with épinards en branche, new potatoes and parsley sauce, it made a pleasant meal.

The first two categories of soybean products would work out no cheaper than eating meat. But nutritionally you are better off. Dishes made at home from the third category would work out very much cheaper than eating meat. Soya flour can be used for baking bread and biscuits and a spoonful can be added to a roux for a white sauce to enrich its protein. One tablespoon of flour has roughly the same food value as an egg.

Soya flakes are dilicious mixed with muesli, added to porridge oats or used in baking. Work on the ratio of one part soya flour or flakes to six parts wholemeal or plain flour.

Soya grits can be used instead of breadcrumbs to roll food in before frying. The grits can also be added to any vegetable croquette mixture, especially one that needs a little firmness. Out of these three you can also make up your own rissole mixture, which works out at about a quarter of the price of the packet varieties.

Soya Rissole Mixture
50 g/2 oz each of grits flakes and flour
2 tablespoons sesame seeds
½ teaspoon celery and garlic salt
2 onions, chopped
2 cloves garlic, crushed
1 egg
140 ml/5 fl oz yoghurt

Mix well together and leave for 5 minutes. Shape and fry in sunflower oil — this amount will make about 8 or 10 rissoles. This mixture is crisp and crunchy; if you want rissoles which are spongier, add a large cup of vegetable purée, potato, spinach or carrot.

Oatmeal biscuits
50 g/2 oz each of the following: oatmeal, soya flakes, soya flour, sesame seeds
100 g/4 oz brown wholemeal flour
1 teaspoon baking powder and sea salt
170 g/6 oz vegetable fat
100 ml/4 fl oz yoghurt

Grate and crumble the fat into the flour and mix with all the dry ingredients. Add yoghurt. Roll out on a floured board. Cut into shapes and cook in a pre-heated oven 350°F/180°C/Gas Mark 4 for 25 minutes.

Thin coconut biscuits
100 g/4 oz wholemeal flour
100 g/4 oz butter
100 g/4 oz desiccated coconut
2 tablespoons soya flour
2 tablespoons brown sugar
A pinch of salt
1 teaspoon baking powder

Mix the butter into the dry ingredients and make a paste. Add 2 tablespoons of water. Use a floured board. Spread the paste thinly over it with your fingers. Cut into biscuit shapes. With a palette knife ease the biscuits off the board and on to a greased baking tray. Cook in a pre-heated oven 350°F/180°C/ Gas Mark 4 for 20 minutes.

Sesame herb bread
4 teaspoons dry yeast
1 teaspoon honey
100 ml/4 fl oz warm water

Mix together and let the yeast start to froth before adding the following:
100 g/4 oz wholemeal flour
75 g/3 oz plain wheatmeal flour
50 g/2 oz soya flour
75 g/3 oz sesame seeds
50 g/2 oz onion, minced
3 teaspoons mixed herbs (marjoram, thyme, dill seeds, ground rosemary, or any others)
100 ml/4 fl oz milk, heated with 25 g/1 oz butter, and 1 teaspoon salt

Add everything to the yeast, stir with a wooden spoon until well mixed, then cover the bowl with a cloth and put somewhere warm for the bread to rise.

When it has tripled in bulk, stir again and tip into a greased bread tin. Sprinkle the top with more sesame seeds. Let it stand again until the dough has risen to the top of the tin, then place in a pre-heated oven 350°F/180°C/Gas Mark 4 for an hour.

SEA VEGETABLES

We tend to be suspicious of seaweed and find the idea of eating it rather comical, but what of sea vegetables? They are perhaps worthy of consideration.

They are, of course, the same thing. Food connoisseurs have dropped the weed as it gives an incorrect image. And if we still insist on ignoring the many varied types of sea vegetables that grow on our own shores, and the others which are imported from Japan, then we are turning our backs on an amazingly cheap and highly nutritious source of food. One, too, which can be delicious, once a few simple basic methods of cooking them have been explored.

Sea vegetables were eaten in the Far East and considered a great delicacy; in the sixth century BC, we have a record of them in China being offered to honoured guests. For centuries in Scotland, Ireland and Norway sea vegetables were gathered, dried, and were a valuable source of minerals and vitamins in the long winter months when no fresh green leaves were available.

The only way the majority of us now eat them is in commercial ice cream where they keep the pig's fat in suspension and prevent the growth of ice crystals; they are also used in soups and salad dressings. They have become important in the food industry, because their mucilaginous substances are used as stabilizers.

They are rich in iodine, potassium, iron, calcium and magnesium; among their many vitamins, they also contain B12, which was thought never to exist in plant foods.

You can get a dozen dishes or more out of one small packet for, once soaked, they expand generously. To the nervous with a sci-fi imagination it can be alarming.

Most wholefood shops now stock a range of sea vegetables imported by Sunwheel Foods. Their shop, Sunwheel Natural Foods in London's Old Street, also stocks dulse and carrageen harvested from the Irish coast, as well as the many sea vegetables imported from Japan. They now have a mail order list, so readers who wish to strike out into tastes and pleasures unknown, or just want a source where they can buy the best quality wholefoods, can write to them at 196 Old Street, London EC1. I think of this shop as the Fortnum and Mason of wholefoods: their products are of impeccable quality and they stock obscure delicacies as well as wonderful condiments that turn the plainest steamed vegetable into Kyoto haute cuisine.

Cooks new to sea vegetables may find the range bewildering. I have listed here the ones that I enjoy most. The cooking methods are all simple if they come already dried out of a packet. If you harvest the sea vegetables from the coast yourself, then the preparation and cooking time will take longer.

Nori sheets
Place a sheet beneath a hot grill and in a few seconds it will bubble and turn green. Crumble it in your fingers and use to sprinkle over food as a condiment. The Japanese use nori sheets to wrap rice balls or to make sushi, which is rice, vegetable or fish, wrapped with nori.

Laver
From the same family as nori. It grows plentifully on the Gower coast in south Wales, also in parts of Scotland, Ireland and Brittany. Gather the laver and wash it under a running tap to remove salt. Leave it soaking in running water for up to three hours. Then boil until soft. It can take anything from two hours to twelve, depending on how young the laver is. It should be as soft as cooked spinach.

60

Drain, then mince the laver into a purée. It will seem very liquid, so mix the purée with enough oatmeal to stiffen it so that it can be shaped into cakes. Then fry in hot olive oil or butter, until brown and crisp.

Kombu
In flavour a little like laver, this is the sea vegetable I use most often. Kelp powder is extracted from it. Soak one or two sticks for about fifteen minutes; they turn into flat bottle-green mucilaginous sheets. Boil in the same water for about another fifteen minutes. You can then spread the cooked sheets with a herb, onion and curd cheese filling, roll as in roulade, then slice across and have them as part of a salad. I also cut the cooked sheets into strips and use as in the *kombu and aduki pâté* recipe below; or throw slices into the wok with stir-fried vegetables; or make the stock and strips of kombu into a clear soup; or use them in casseroles with beans.

Arame
This looks like black bootlaces. Soak for five minutes, then boil until soft (about ten minutes). Drain and deep fry in sunflower oil until crisp. Or, after boiling, add a tablespoon of shoyu or tamari soy sauce, add a handful of chopped spring onions and use as a sauce for buckwheat spaghetti. Can also be added to stir-fried vegetables.

Wakame
This comes in long curly strands with a centre vein which must be cut out and discarded. Can be eaten after it has been soaked and sliced finely, with other vegetables in a salad.

Carrageen
This grows in Ireland, and can be used as a vegetable gelatin. Wash it in running water for an hour then boil for thirty minutes in water or milk, strain the liquid, flavour it with either a savoury vegetable stock, or fruit juice and sherry and use as a basis for a dessert. Carrageen can be

bought in packets. Carrageen jellies and drinks were once considered necessary fare for invalids.

Dulse
When dried, dulse was chewed, it is said, by the Irish like tobacco. Icelanders today chew pepper dulse. Dried dulse in packets can be soaked for five minutes, then finely sliced and added to salads, or deep fried in batter, or used with stir-fried vegetables.

Kombu and Aduki Bean Pâté

170 g/6 oz dried aduki beans
2 sticks soaked kombu
100 g/4 oz mixed ground nuts
2 eggs
8 bay leaves
1 teaspoon dried ground rosemary
2 tablespoons natural soy sauce

Soak aduki beans overnight. Boil in the same water, with 4 of the bay leaves, either in the pressure cooker for half an hour or in a saucepan for an hour. The beans must be soft enough to mash or shove through a sieve, so that they become a chunky purée. Discard cooked bay leaves.

Meanwhile, cook the kombu sheets in the water they have soaked in for about ten minutes. Leave to cool. Cut kombu into 1 cm/½ inch squares, add to the purée with 140 ml/5 fl oz water it has cooked in. Add the ground nuts, rosemary, soy sauce, mix well, then add the 2 beaten eggs. Taste and season.

Lay the 4 remaining bay leaves in a design at the bottom of a well greased terrine dish, pate or bread tin. Pour the mixture into the tin and bake in a pre-heated oven at 425°F/218°C/Gas Mark 7 for 30 minutes or until a knife plunged into the centre comes out clean. Leave to cool overnight.

To turn out: place the bottom of the dish into hot water for a moment, then upturn over a platter. Serve sliced. You will find that the kombu has patterned the pate obligingly as if it were truffles. What is more important, the taste is far superior to those bits of tinned truffle resembling flakes of patent leather. Is it not about time that food manufacturers scrutinized the gourmet potential in sea vegetables?

BREAD

The National Housewives' Association is angry about bread. They have been angry about bread for years and they are getting angrier as unemployment rises. Yet Britain's two big bakers, Associated British Foods and Rank Hovis McDougall, appear sanguine about the anger.

The Chorleywood Process researchers, who advise on the type of seeds planted, the grain milled and the kind of bread baked, dismiss the anger of the Association and others as in no way typical of the population. They claim that they have produced exactly the bread the customers want. Is it feasible that those rectangles of cotton lint were a market demand? (There are eleven different chemicals added to white flour, including several that bleach.) Surely it must have been like that kids' whispering game where the message at the end is a total distortion of the original statement.

According to the *Sunday Times Books of Real Bread* (edited by Heather Maisner and Michael Bateman), a white tasteless dough is preferred by the Chorleywood researchers themselves. They say anyone who likes wholemeal is at the gourmet end of the market, and they believe, belongs to a tiny minority led by Elizabeth David.

The statistics prove them wrong. Over the last ten years the consumption of wholemeal bread in the lowest income group has more than doubled. The National Housewives' Association rightly consider bread as a staple food; wholemeal bread provides a family with essential nutrients which can be the satisfying half of a square meal. When members of that family are unemployed it is essential that

63

bread should be cheap, nutritious and filling. When the bread tastes good, you do not need to smother it with butter or much else. But this is exactly the kind of good bread that the big bakers will not provide.

Why not? Eighteen per cent of us now demand wholemeal, which costs more, though it ought to cost less, as it has not been processed into white bread. This is the missing crunch, so what happens to it? The bran, wheatgerm, vitamins and minerals removed from the white bread are used for animal feed, called in the trade 'offal'; this is sold by Rank Hovis McDougall as highly nutritious food for pigs and poultry and for cereals in canned pet foods. A significant proportion of the cost of the wheat is recouped by selling the offal. So if Big Brother Baker makes more wholemeal bread for us they have less offal to sell and there is a decline in profits.

Associated British Foods and Rank Hovis McDougall were behind a one-and-a-half-million-pound advertising campaign based around the health image of bread given by a report commissioned by the DHSS. The report continually stressed the dietary fibre virtues of bran in the wholemeal, but advertising continually plugs the nutritional riches of all bread, even that pathetic object, the white sliced loaf.

Thankfully we have a choice: bake our own. It is not difficult. It has to be done in stages and the dough can be left to rise all night, or all day while you are out. There is something magical about yeast (wild yeasts exist in the air around us) and once you start making your own bread, it quickly becomes compulsive. When I make a herb loaf for a dinner party of six, it has vanished by the end of the meal.

The *Book of Real Bread* encourages home baking. It is a celebration of bread in a multiplicity of its most desirable forms. The book gives you a history of bread and the state of play now, it goes into simple and precise detail on methods of kneading, rising and baking. It tells you where to buy good flours, lists various glazes and finishes, goes into equipment (you hardly need any) and gives you a guide of British mills. But the bulk of the book is recipes from people who bake their own bread. They are fascinating and delicious, proof of the infinite variety of breads with flavour and crust.

Another book of indispensable value for the home baker is *English Bread and Yeast Cookery* by Elizabeth David (Penguin), a book to read with immense enjoyment as well as to cook from. Mrs David says in the *Book of Real Bread* that every school should have courses in bread-making (as in Denmark), then some of the young would discriminate between good and bad bread. Like much else, it comes down to education: society belts out the message that the white sliced loaf is real bread, and the majority believe it. So, it would seem, do the Chorleywood researchers, who look upon our demand for real bread as a fashionable phase that will soon fade away.

The recipe below needs no kneading. If you add enough water so that the consistency of the dough is both tacky and fluid, the loaf will be deliciously moist and will be one of the lightest wholemeal loaves you are ever likely to eat. The point about this recipe is that you are adding other high protein ingredients which flavour the flour. This is my favourite bread recipe and I eat the loaf, either fresh or toasted, almost every day.

High Protein Loaf (Makes 3 loaves)
1 kg/2¼lb wholemeal flour
15 g/½oz dried yeast (or 25 g/1 oz fresh yeast)
825 ml to 1 litre 1½ pints to 2 pints water
1 teaspoon salt
3 tablespoons crushed wheat
3 tablespoons bran
3 tablespoons soya flour
4 tablespoons wheat germ
3 tablespoons linseeds
3 tablespoons sesame seeds
1 tablespoon dried brewer's yeast
4 tablespoons skimmed milk powder
3 tablespoons olive oil

Add a little of the water, after it has been warmed, to the yeast in a large bowl. For this amount you will need a very large bowl if you are mixing the dough by hand. If you are using an electric dough hook, then you will have to divide these amounts into 3 and mix the ingredients for the 3 loaves separately.

When the yeast has begun to work on the water — that is, froth and bubble a little — add the rest of the dry ingredients and mix well. Add the rest of the warmed water gradually. Once you get a dough which is elastic it means the yeast is working throughout; at that point add more of the water, so that it is impossible to knead, even if you should want to. Consistency should be a thick mixture, like a stiff Indian dhal. If there is not enough water added, the loaf will turn out hard and heavy.

Oil 3 bread tins, pour the mixture into the tins and place them in large plastic bags in a warm place to rise. Pre-heat oven to 450°F/230°C/Gas Mark 8 and bake the risen loaves in the oven for fifteen minutes, then lower the heat to 350°F/175°C/Gas Mark 6 for a further twenty minutes.

BROWN RICE

Brown rice is the only rice to eat. I use long-grain rice and cook 300 g/10 oz of rice to 550 ml/1 pint of water. Bring water to the boil, drop the rice in, give it a stir, bring back to the boil, place the lid on the pan firmly and leave over a low heat for forty to forty-five minutes when the rice will have absorbed all the water. This amount of rice is enough for 6 people.

Many cooks use a pressure cooker for brown rice, and use it successfully; so far I have failed to control both the timing and the pressure, so that the rice has been either overcooked or underdone. I have found macrobiotic cookery books to be unhelpful in their advice over this problem. They also frown on brown rice being used as leftovers, except in rice balls. I have discovered that brown rice the following day is, if anything, rather nicer than fresh; you can fry it in sesame oil with garlic and a few nuts or strands of seaweed, or you can mix it up with an egg and stir-fry the rice.

MEALS IN A HURRY

I was asked for ideas for a meal for someone tired and in a hurry — and whose local shops have shut. It must be quick, satisfying, but meatless; not centred on eggs and not a snack. A tall order you might think. But the request is more basic than it seems. We all want good everyday food and imaginative ideas which do not take ages to prepare. But it also has to be food which costs little, is fresh and wholesome and has not been refined, textured, flaked, spun, condensed, juiced, canned or frozen. My demanding friend says that when he entertains or plans a menu there are no problems; the beans are soaked, the chick peas blended, dough proved and the yoghurt made.

But for most of the time we are not entertaining, giving dinner parties with selective recipes. We cater for ourselves or small families and it is becoming more and more difficult to resist the superficial charms of some convenience foods.

When I am feeling particularly feeble I almost, but not quite, believe what the advertisements tell me. So it is for those evenings of exhaustion that we should plan with some of the considered thought that we spend on entertaining. The problem is we never quite know when they are going to occur and it is this uncertainty which stops us planning ahead. Perhaps we should just acknowledge that we are bound to feel feeble at least once, and maybe twice, a week and plan accordingly.

What we are seeking is a range of food that is partially prepared at the weekend, which is then kept in the refrigerator, covered, and which in a matter of minutes can easily be made in a variety of attractive meals.

Divide the components of the meals into three: cereals, dried pulses, fresh vegetables. Under the cereals we have a choice of white or brown rice, bulgar wheat, millet, couscous and others. Pulses: flageolet, haricot, lima and butter beans (I am merely picking out from the range my own favourites); green lentils, split peas and mung beans. Fresh vegetables: whatever is in season. But the recipes below are for the winter months.

Choose a different cereal or pulse every week and cook the amount you might need. 100 g/4 oz uncooked rice, millet or bulgar wheat makes enough for at least two meals. By trial and error you will know how many dried beans or peas to cook, but I would have thought the same amount was about right.

You never have to prepare red or yellow lentils in advance, as they need no soaking and will cook through within fifteen minutes. It is the cereals, beans and the freshness of the vegetables which our diet tends to be lowest in, for institutional, canteen or pub lunches are sparing with these foods.

Say it is a week when you have brown rice and lima beans already prepared. The menu could be lentil and bean soup followed by stir-fried vegetables with rice; or steamed vegetables with rice and bean croquettes; or a vegetable pilau; or a vegetable and bean soup followed by brown rice with sesame sauce (see page 70) or stir-fried ginger and tofu. Once you start, the permutations seem endless and the same follows with the millet or bulgar wheat instead of the rice.

Brown rice needs to cook in boiling water, simmered over a low heat for one hour. Both millet and bulgar wheat need dry roasting at first: place grains in a saucepan over a flame, shake the pan to stop the grains sticking. When they smell nutty and have turned a shade of gold they are done. Add enough water to cover, then simmer for up to 30 minutes.

I have taken it for granted that you have your own favourite staple foods in the store cupboard. I would have dried mushrooms and sea vegetables, olive oil, miso paste, tofu, sesame salt, shoyu (natural soy sauce) as well as herbs and spices. In winter, it is not a bad thing to soak dried apricots, peaches, or nectarines and to have those in the refrigerator as well. These can be chopped up and added to the cereal and vegetables or just eaten as a dessert.

Millet Casserole for 2
100 g/4 oz dried millet
1 tablespoon olive oil
1 green pepper, 3 leeks, and 3 celery stalks
2 crushed cloves of garlic
275 ml/10 fl oz water
sea salt or sesame salt to taste

The millet casserole is the simplest recipe: you can add whatever vegetables and spices you prefer. If using this method, then you would cook the millet separately at the weekend. On returning home you chop the vegetables, crush the garlic and sauté it in the oil for about 5 minutes, then add the millet and let it soak up all the oil and juices. Cooking time — 10 minutes.

If you haven't prepared ahead, pour the millet into a saucepan for dry roasting. In another pan put the oil, chopped vegetables and garlic, and sauté for a moment before adding the dry roasted millet and the water. Let it simmer for 30 minutes or until the millet has puffed up and soaked up all the liquids.

Steamed celery with dill
1 head celery
140 ml/5 fl oz water
1 teaspoon dill weed
1 tablespoon shoyu

Wash and chop celery into bite-size pieces. Place into a saucepan with the water, dill weed, and shoyu. Cook over a moderate heat for about 10 minutes or until all the liquid has been absorbed.

Sesame sauce
4 tablespoons sesame spread or tahini
Juice from 1 lemon
4 tablespoons water

Combine everything, mixing well until it goes smooth and creamy.

A LAST WORD

I have never believed that cooking is a difficult art to learn. But what I have come to realize is that good creative cooking, of whatever kind, stems from a certain frame of mind, a certain sensibility that is in harmony with life.

We all know from our experience that dishes do not work if they have been cooked when we are angry, bitter, or resentful, and the times that we live in often exacerbate these negative emotions. A successful dish stems from a contented cook, not the content that derives from apathy or smugness, but the content which is an expression of a certain philosophical serenity. It is, of course, the cooking which expresses love, concern and care for family and friends. How can this cooking, I wonder, ever be based upon the graveyard remnants of a once living creature?

For you cannot be in harmony with life and exploit other living creatures by trapping them, imprisoning them, taking new-born away from lactating mothers, allowing the babies a few days of life in a tiny crate so small it is impossible to move an inch, over-feeding the young so that within a year they have diseases of the liver and heart, injecting them with a range of powerful drugs and ignoring the side effects on the animals and the carcass.

Your own body will respond gratefully to a new healthy vegetarian diet; they are affable companions and will adjust easily. You will find that the body builds up a greater resistance to diseases, you will have more natural energy and you will sleep sounder.

70

Spring

With what relief we feel the first warmth of an early spring day! Almost at once the body seems to demand fresh salads and green leaves, but for our own garden vegetables we still have to wait for late May and June. I am truly grateful for the first herbs (see pages 31-33). Without those we have to rely on the imported lettuces (our own hot-house ones or those that come from Holland are bland and indigestible); those varieties which are all crisp heart are worth buying. They keep wrapped in cling film in the refrigerator for many days quite happily, if you do not break off the stalk. A good lettuce needs no other chopped vegetable with it, but it will need imaginative salad dressings.

Experiment with various flavoured wine and rice vinegars. Use a flavoured oil like sesame, peanut or walnut. You will only need a little sesame oil stirred into another oil to bequeath the salad that hint of flavour. Here are some suggestions:

Sesame Salad Dressing
1 teaspoon toasted sesame oil
2 tablespoons corn oil
1 tablespoon rice vinegar
1 teaspoon sesame salt

Mix all thoroughly together.

Walnut salad dressing
1 tablespoon walnut oil
2 tablespoons sunflower oil
1 tablespoon cider vinegar
pinch of sea salt and freshly ground black pepper
1 tablespoon crushed walnuts

Mix all thoroughly together.

Mustard salad dressing
2 teaspoons good dijon mustard
1 teaspoon honey
2 tablespoons olive oil
1 teaspoon cider vinegar
Pinch of sea salt and freshly ground black pepper

Mix all thoroughly together.

Shake or stir all the dressings well before pouring them over the salad, and take time tossing the salad, so that every leaf is covered with a film of the flavoured oil.

Enjoy salads where the vegetables are cooked *al dente*. Make your own mayonnaise; I do regard this as essential. Besides, I have a great fondness for making mayonnaise with the old method of a bowl and a wooden spoon, rather than using the liquidizer. I am convinced that the mayonnaise tastes superior.

There is a lot of snobbery about mayonnaise. Some believe that it should only be made from olive oil and never, as is the French habit, begun by thickening the egg yolks with a little powdered mustard. I disagree. Try this method and discover how easy and fulfilling making mayonnaise can be.

Mayonnaise
2 egg yolks
$\frac{1}{2}$ teaspoon powdered mustard
$\frac{1}{4}$ pint olive oil
$\frac{1}{4}$ pint sunflower oil
$\frac{1}{2}$ teaspoon salt

Make sure that the eggs are at room temperature. If they are taken straight from the refrigerator, the mayonnaise will curdle; so, unlike pastry where everything has to be chilled, both egg yolks and oil should be left for a few hours in a comfortable temperature in the kitchen.

Separate yolks from whites. Take a deep bowl (a 2 pint pudding basin is fine) and place it on a firm table. Stir the mustard into the yolks in the bowl. Pour the two oils into one jug. Have ready a wooden spoon or a whisk; start pouring the oil drop by drop into the yolks and mustard and stir the oil quickly. You have to work fast, in the sense that each drop of oil must be quickly absorbed. After about 2 tablespoons of oil has gone in, the emulsion should now have thickened. It will then get thicker as you add the rest of the $\frac{1}{2}$ pint of oil. The 2 egg yolks can take twice the amount of oil, but one rarely needs that amount of mayonnaise — though it will keep beautifully in a screw-top jar for a week or more, (not in the refrigerator because oil and yolks will separate). Add the salt at the last moment. If the mayonnaise is too thick, you can add about a teaspoon of lemon juice mixed with the same amount of water. This gives it a lovely flavour and a light colour.

Use yoghurt as a *salad dressing*. Mix 2 tablespoons of yoghurt, 1 crushed clove of garlic, the juice from 1 lemon and 1 tablespoon of olive oil, a pinch of sea salt and black pepper. This is excellent for cauliflower salad.

Try grating vegetables other than the usual cabbage and carrot: grated courgettes, raw beetroot, celeriac, young turnip. The latter makes a lovely salad, if lightly cooked in thin slices, then tossed in a little vinaigrette sauce (see page 96 for a suitable one; I use it for avocados).

With luck the first spinach leaves can be picked early on and these make an excellent salad, especially with sliced avocado. Cold bean salads are also good. If you choose red kidney beans (see pages 150-51), flageolet and black beans, they can look spectacular arranged in a large bowl, kept apart to show the variations of colour. Flavour each variety after it has been cooked. The beans need to be tossed, while still warm, in a little olive oil with a different herb or spice: flageolets can be tossed in oil and chopped parsley or mint; the red kidney beans in oil and paprika, the black beans in oil and grated root ginger.

Or what about stir-fried vegetables? There is, in my opinion, no better way of cooking vegetables to preserve their flavour and nutritious value, if it is done correctly.

It is intriguing how food manufacturers get in on current trends fairly quickly, but then get it hopelessly wrong. Marks and Spencer now stock in their frozen food department stir-fried vegetables. The packets contain courgettes, onions, sweetcorn, and peas, and there is another type which has cauliflower instead of the courgettes.

The point about stir-fried vegetables, as everyone knows who has eaten at a Chinese restaurant enjoyed by the Chinese themselves, is that the vegetables are hearty chunks, their exterior sealed by succulent oils and flavourings while their centre is raw, juicy and distinctly chewable. M & S must have been considering the inhabitants of a dolls house, or else their slicing machine went berserk and like an echo of Modern Times could not be halted. For the vegetables have been reduced to decimal points of insignificance, I swear even the peas have been quartered. (M & S excuse themselves by saying that their packets of stir-fried vegetables omit the word 'Chinese'. However, they do admit that 'stir-fried is a term we associate with Chinese cuisine'.)

Given the fact that Chinese cooking is as much an art as the French cuisine, is it worth having a bash at it at home? No doubt about it, I would say, though I think it worth while investing in a wok. You can stir-fry in a frying pan but a wok achieves the authentic flavour with far more ease; the only skill you need is to work out carefully the timing of each vegetable and each part of a vegetable;

broccoli and cauliflower stalks, for example, need several minutes cooking while the flowerets only one minute. Preparation is essential, and three quarters of the battle. The actual cooking can be done in five minutes. But much of the art lies in the preparation, how and what to slice, and in the choice of vegetables.

Peas and sweetcorn are unsuitable for stir-frying, they just are not big enough. So choose vegetables that have to be sliced, exposing the tenderest parts. Choose the freshest and the best part of a vegetable, that part of it which you would probably eat and enjoy raw anyway. It is no good thinking you can work a miracle on some jaded part of a vegetable, bouncing it around a hot wok in walnut oil and grated ginger. It will look and taste even more dismal after that treatment.

You will have to consider the characteristics of each vegetable and slice accordingly; always remember when slicing that you must uncover the greatest possible area of the vegetable to the heat. That is why the Chinese slice diagonally, not just to make it look pretty; though their eye for aesthetics is sharp, and they have a nice talent for colour range and combinations which is worth borrowing. (Macrobiotic cooking also slices diagonally, in order that each segment of the vegetable has parts of the whole vegetable in it: this reflects the unity of the original form.) Green peppers and lettuce will be much brightened by the Corot touch of slivers of red carrot.

Never dump into the wok too many different kinds of vegetables (this is my failing, and I have to watch it). Three is enough, with the additional flavourings; the wok should not be more than half full at the beginning, otherwise it is impossible for all the pieces of vegetable to cook at the same rate. It is best to cut, peel and slice each vegetable and line them up in the order of cooking time. Remember that a diagonal sliver of carrot or a 5 cm/2 inch chunk of celery will not take longer than four minutes, so you will need everything at hand, including any spices and flavourings. My choice of vegetables below is quite arbitrary; you might just as well have cabbage, spinach and celery, or any other combination.

Stir-fried vegetables
250 g/½ lb broccoli
2 green peppers
2 onions
2 cloves of crushed garlic
25 g/1 oz grated ginger root
2 tablespoons peanut or sunflower oil

Cut the flowerets from the broccoli and lightly peel the stalks. Cut the peppers in half, core them, slice them in ½ cm by 5 cm/¼ inch by 2 inch lengths. Quarter the onions — they will fall into smaller pieces as they cook. Heat the wok on its stand with the oil, garlic, and grated ginger root and allow them to flavour the oil (they will need to cook for a minute or two, but watch that they don't burn). Throw in the green peppers and the broccoli stalks and move them constantly around the wok, so that all pieces are being evenly cooked and covered in the oil.

You will need a high heat to seal all the surfaces and keep the interior juices from leaking. (Same principle as the bleu grilling of a steak.) After 2 minutes throw in the onions, cook for another minute and a half or thereabouts, then add the broccoli flowerets. Go on stirring and shoving the pieces up and around the wok for not longer than a minute. Serve immediately.

You could garnish with spring onions or sprinkle flaked almonds over the dish in the last seconds; you could also add, in the last half minute of cooking, one of the Chinese flavourings. Chinese stores stock them and many are delicious, for they are the same ones as used in the restaurants. Satay, five spices powder, sesame paste, yellow or black bean paste and hoisin sauce are some of many, but beware for there are others (including most commercial brands of soy sauce) which are synthetic, not brewed naturally and fermented for many months. Wholefood shops now stock a most delicious and pure soy sauce called tamari. It is alas, more expensive, but well worth it; indispensable for the following recipe.

Poached bean sprouts and lettuce
Large cos or small Chinese lettuce
225 g/½ lb bean sprouts
1 tablespoon olive oil
25 g/1 oz butter
1 glass dry sherry
140 ml/¼ pint vegetable stock
1 tablespoon tamari sauce
1 level teaspoon cornflour

Melt butter and olive oil in a saucepan over a low heat. Tear each leaf of the lettuce into two or three and throw (a gesture both nonchalant and precise) into the saucepan with the sherry. Place the lid on it and let it steam and reduce for about two minutes. When it is half its bulk add the bean sprouts, half of the vegetable stock and the tamari sauce. Let it cook for another minute. Mix cornflour with the rest of the stock and add to the vegetables. Stir quickly until it is thickened slightly. The vegetables should be *al dente*, serve immediately.

Of the great cuisines of the world, the French and the Chinese, I much prefer the latter. In both cuisines as a vegetarian you can eat supremely well. But the Chinese stir-fry method of cooking vegetables ensures a minimum loss of vitamins and minerals and there is the choice of what seems an almost limitless range of sauces and spices which can transform a dish into an epicure's dream. But over this amazingly varied cuisine there hangs a spectre: monosodium glutamate, or MSG.

A friend, a Dutch sculptress, once committed a malapropism by referring to MSG as glutinous sodomites. She was complaining of MSG being used in a large range of tinned and frozen foods consumed by us in the West. MSG can be addictive, and it can make some people ill with a painful flushing in the face (this may occur after eating at a Chinese restaurant), but, it would be an inferior cook who would use large amounts of MSG. Its intense savoury flavour is always immediately apparent and to most of us nauseating.

There is now almost a crusade against the use of MSG. But like everything else, it would be wise to arm ourselves with a few facts before arriving at a judgement. MSG occurs naturally in fermented soy sauce, and is the sodium salt of one of the amino acids. In ancient China it was derived from the fermentation of wheat and seaweeds, but is now often made from sugar beet molasses. It stimulates the taste buds, but too much whizzes up the sinuses and causes the flushing. In tiny children an excess could cause brain damage. In the USA, baby food manufacturers are now banned from using it in their products.

I would dearly like to see our own food manufacturers omit it altogether from their list of additives. Birds Eye stir-fried vegetables, for example, taste of nothing else, and we have no way of checking how much MSG we are consuming every day in packet soup, frozen foods and tins.

But I admit that I have kept a jar of MSG (sometimes called taste powder, flavouring salt, or as the Chinese call it, Ve-Tsin) on a shelf in the pantry for many years and I occasionally use a pinch of it. The point is to use it and not to depend upon it. If you add MSG yourself you are in control of the amount of it you consume. So while I would deplore manufactured foods containing MSG, I sometimes find it essential in stir-fried dishes on Chinese cooking.

For many years I have relied on Chinese stores for spices, now, however, Sharwood's have brought out a range of authentic Chinese provisions which can be purchased in supermarkets and some delicatessens.

There is no MSG in their sauces, but there is one tin

which is MSG and flavouring vegetable salts. So it is your choice whether you use MSG or not.

In Chinese cooking there are three basic rules to remember. First, prepare all the food in advance and cut it roughly to the same size. Secondly, ensure that the wok is very hot, so that it almost begins to glow. Thirdly, toss the food around the wok for a few minutes only, never allowing the vegetables to lose their slight crispness.

Cos lettuce in yellow bean sauce

1 cos lettuce
1 tablespoon sunflower oil
1 teaspoon Sharwood's sesame oil
2 tablespoons Sharwood's Yellow Bean sauce

Tear the lettuce into pieces roughly the size of a tablespoon. Heat the wok. Pour sunflower and sesame oil in, throw in all of the lettuce and toss for about one minute, so that all pieces just begin to shrivel. Take the wok from the heat and add the Yellow Bean sauce, place the wok back on the heat and toss again, so that the sauce covers the lettuce.

Chow mein

1 packet of noodles
2 tablespoons sunflower oil
2 green peppers, finely sliced
2 carrots, in julienne strips
2 onions, cut coarsely
4 tablespoons Sharwood's Black Bean and Chilli sauce

Place noodles in boiling water, bring back to the boil, pop a lid on the saucepan and take away from the heat.

Heat the wok, pour in the sunflower oil. Throw in the carrots and toss for about half a minute, add the peppers and onions, continue tossing for another minute or perhaps two. They should just begin to get a little soft, that is all. Now add the sauce and toss again.

Drain the noodles and add them to the wok. Mix thoroughly and serve.

EGGS

I have a particular fondness for *oeuf mollet*. We have no English word for the arrested cooking in a boiled egg. *Mollet* describes an egg which stops cooking when the white is firm and the yolk is still raw, or runny. Soft-boiled is the nearest equivalent, but is not as precise as *mollet*.

Oeuf Mollet provides us with some of the most delicious ways of beginning a meal. Served in individual ramekin dishes (or cocottes) the soft-boiled eggs, springy to a light-fingered touch, lie on a delicate vegetable purée and are glazed with a sauce. Delicious hot or cold, in either case they can be prepared for a dinner party some hours beforehand, leaving one free to tackle the main course.

But it is necessary to have a strict regimen and timing to achieve the right result. First choose a pan in which the eggs will fit, so that you can wedge them in without moving. Wire egg holders do exist, in which you place the eggs before lowering them into the water. It sounds a perfect answer to the problem — and I still have not acquired one.

For a large egg to be *mollet* it must be boiled for three and a half minutes and not a second more. Standard eggs need three minutes. Have your eggs at room temperature, wedge them into the saucepan and pour the boiling water down the side of the pan to cover them. If you pour the boiling water straight on to the eggs they will crack. If an egg still cracks you will have to dispense with it and start again. Place the saucepan immediately over the heat, so that the water quietly simmers, and you can start timing. When the time is up, plunge the eggs into a basin of cold water, or let the cold tap run over them. They must stop cooking. If you just drain the water from them, there is enough heat in the egg to cook the yolk through.

Most recipes for *oeuf mollet* give a timing of four minutes for the cooking. But the minute they are immersed in boiling water they begin to cook a little, and certainly there is a fraction of time to be allowed for after they are immersed in cold water. If even half of the yolk is cooked through, there is in my terms, no point in *mollet*, because the whole enjoyment of the dish is the flavour of the raw yolk fusing with the purée and sauces.

Allow the eggs to cool. It is almost impossible to peel the shell from an egg still angry with heat, which is why *oeuf mollet* hot is more difficult to contrive. With the back of a teaspoon gently beat the egg so that hair cracks appear, peel the shell with its inner membrane away and with luck the whole shell will fall away like a jacket.

If you want your *mollet* hot, have the ramekins warming up in the oven, and the vegetable purée hot in a saucepan. Spoon purée into each ramekin, place the egg on to it. Have the ramekins standing in a baking dish, pour boiling water into the dish and pop it in to the oven for about 3 minutes or until the eggs are just heated through. Any longer and the yolks will begin to cook. Meanwhile, make your sauce, or reheat it to cover the tops of the eggs. Pour a little of the sauce into each ramekin and serve immediately.

Here are some suggestions for purées and sauces.

Leek purée
600 g/1 lb 5 oz leeks
25 g/1 oz butter
Seasoning

Trim the leeks, split wash and cut them across in 1 cm/½ inch slices, then pop them into a saucepan with the butter over a low heat. Place the lid on and leave them for a few minutes. They will steam in their own liquid and should be cooked within 3 minutes. Let them cool, then liquidize. Add seasoning, check by tasting. Place enough purée in each ramekin to cover the base by 1 cm/½ inch. Enough to serve 5. An *onion purée* is made the same way.

Caper sauce
25 g/1 oz butter
140 ml/5 fl oz water
2 tablespoons capers
Glass dry sherry
½ teaspoon cornflour

Melt the butter and add the drained capers. Let them sweat in the butter, then add the water, bring to the boil and simmer for a moment. Add sherry, simmer for another moment, then thicken with cornflour. Pour over each egg in its ramekin.

Potato purée
600 g/1 lb potatoes
50 g/2 oz butter
2 tablespoons double cream
Sea salt and freshly ground black pepper

Peel and boil the potatoes. Drain, then put the pan back over the heat and stir for a moment, so that any excess water is driven off in steam. Shove all the potatoes through a sieve, add the butter, mix well, add salt, pepper and cream, stir again. Enough here for about 8 ramekins.

Mustard and egg sauce
2 cooked egg yolks
1 raw egg yolk
3 teaspoons moutarde de meaux (or mustard powder)
140 ml/5 fl oz double cream

Make a paste of the cooked egg yolks and the mustard, add the raw yolk, a pinch of salt and stir in the cream.

All the above purées and sauces can be eaten hot or cold (except for the potato, which is not very nice cold). You can make purées of mushroom spinach, aubergine, avocado, even of the plebeian parsnip, though I would be tempted to use a few curry spices with it. You can also cover the egg with a simple béchamel or mornay sauce. Almost any sauce or purée will merge happily with *oeuf mollet*.

It is a sign of a good restaurant if they cook their *oeufs en cocotte* perfectly, so that the whites are done, and the yolks uncooked. I have always found it impossible to judge the timing if the eggs are baked in their ramekin dishes in the oven. But cooking them in a water bath on top of the stove is child's play.

Oeufs en cocotte pascal
1 egg per person
Handful chopped parsley and chives
Few sprigs of tarragon
2 teaspoons moutarde de meaux
Pinch of sea salt
Black pepper
4 tablespoons thick cream

Cook the eggs in buttered china ramekins, which resemble small soufflé dishes. Place the ramekins in a pan of quietly simmering water, slip an egg into each dish, cover the pan and leave for 3 minutes.

Have the following sauce ready: chop the parsley, chives and sprigs of tarragon, place in a pan with the moutarde de meaux, or a fine mustard of your choice, a pinch of sea salt, a few grinds of freshly-milled pepper and the cream. Stir well, heat carefully, then pour it over the cooked eggs.

SPINACH

My generation and the one before were brought up on spinach, as if it was a miracle food. If only we consumed enough of it, all our ills would fade away. It was, of course, the days of Popeye the Sailor Man as a comic strip hero who, we read every day, performed feats of Herculean strength and possessed arms suffering from advanced elephantiasis. None of this affected me much, as I genuinely liked spinach. Thankfully it was before the days of frozen spinach, so we only ate it in the early summer months, fresh from the garden.

The earliest mention of spinach is in AD 647 in China where it was called the herb of Persia, where it is thought to have originated. The Arabs brought it to Spain in the twelfth century. From there, it spread slowly north through those monastic gardens where so much of what we now eat was nurtured. The monks grew it for its supposedly medicinal qualities. It is a mild laxative.

In the earlier part of this century it was considered good for us, as it was rich in Vitamins A and C, iron and calcium. But like sorrel, which it resembles when growing, it is high in oxalic acid which combines with the minerals to form insoluble oxalates. This means that the so-called 'goodness' is never released to be digested. This, alas, must be the reason why the muscles of our limbs remained a modest size.

We can now appreciate spinach just for its own deliciousness. the best way of dealing with it is to eat it as young and fresh as possible, to tear leaf from stalk, and either cook them separately or, if the stalks tend to be at all fibrous, throw them out for the compost.

The recipes here are for the leaves only. Never allow spinach to touch water after it is clean. Let the leaves drain in a colander after they have been washed, then squeeze or shake them dryer still. Place in a saucepan with a knob of butter and let the leaves cook over a moderate heat in their own steam. Lift the lid once after two minutes and give the leaves a stir, or push the uncooked leaves down to the bottom. Spinach should be cooked within five minutes. Drain off any excess liquid, or raise heat and let the liquid evaporate. With this method of cooking there may not be any liquid at all. Add a little sea salt and freshly ground pepper at the end of cooking. This is spinach *en branche*, and needs only to be served with a little more butter.

For a purée, put the cooked spinach into a blender and liquidize for a moment; too long will make it too liquid. Two tablespoons of this purée can be added to a mayonnaise with a little sorrel and parsley to make *sauce verte* (green sauce).

Some of the purée can be added to a béchamel sauce with 25 g/1 oz of freshly-grated parmesan as a green sauce for cauliflower or other steamed vegetables. The strong mineral taste of spinach can be adjusted with the addition of cheeses, cream, yoghurt, and eggs.

My distaste for frozen spinach is because its water content seems greater than its leaf content. The cooking time on the packet will often reduce the leaves to a few teaspoons only suitable for a garnish.

The first spinach salad I ever ate was in a restaurant; the leaves were small, but tough. It put me off trying raw spinach again for years. The leaves must be young and tender.

Spinach and avocado salad
450 g/1 lb young spinach leaves
25 g/1 oz grated parmesan
2 chopped hard-boiled eggs
50 g/2 oz garlic croutons
2 avocados
Juice from 1 lemon
2 tablespoons olive oil
2 teaspoons ground roasted sesame seeds
Sea salt and freshly-ground black pepper

Use at least three cloves of garlic to make the croutons; set them aside. Slice the avocados in two, take the stone out and peel the skin away, dice the flesh. Put into a bowl and add all the other ingredients except for the spinach and croutons. Mix well. Tear the spinach from the centre stalks, wash and pat dry in a clean cloth. Spread the spinach leaves out in a salad bowl, heap the avocado mixture in the centre. Sprinkle the croutons over the lot.

Buttered spinach

1 kg/2¼ lb spinach
675 g/1½ lb butter

Yes, the amount of butter is terrifying, but the completed dish is an amazing delicacy. Cook the spinach as already suggested in only a knob of butter, then squeeze all the moisture from the leaves through a colander. Melt 225 g/8 oz of the butter in the saucepan and return the spinach to it. Stir with a wooden spoon and almost grind the spinach into the butter as it cooks. The spinach will soon soak up all the butter. Refrigerate for a day.

The following day repeat the cooking process. Use another 225 g/8 oz butter and cook, stirring hard, until the spinach has soaked all of it up. On the third day, repeat the process with the same amount of butter. As soon as the butter is hot, the whole process should take no longer than three minutes. Once the spinach has soaked up the butter on the first day it never reduces in bulk, it should still be just *en branche* but a slight purée as well. (Readers may well think that the inclusion of this recipe is irresponsible madness. However, if your butter intake has been minimal for many months, eating a portion of this dish — the amount is enough for six people — is only the equivalent of a syllabub or dish of profiteroles with whipped cream. Cookery writers cannot legislate for individuals.)

Macaroni with spinach

170 g/6 oz macaroni
450 g/1 lb spinach reduced to a purée (see above)
100 g/4 oz mozzarella cheese
225 g/½ lb grated sage derby cheese
275 ml/½ pint sauce béchamel
50 g/2 oz grated parmesan cheese
2 tablespoons breadcrumbs
Sea salt and freshly-ground pepper

Butter a soufflé dish and pour the spinach purée into it. Cut the mozzarella into 2½ cm/1 inch cubes and dot it over the spinach. Mix the sage derby with the béchamel sauce, and season. Boil the macaroni until it is *al dente*; drain well, and combine with the sauce. Pour it over the spinach, sprinkle with the grated parmesan and breadcrumbs. Bake in a pre-heated oven 350°F/ 175°C/Gas Mark 4 for 25 minutes, or until the sauce is bubbling and the top is crisp.

QUICHE

The name quiche covers many a tart or flan, though if you are a purist it should apply only to quiche Lorraine which contains cream, eggs, bacon, and no cheese. However, as humanity is far from pure, the word quiche now means to us vegetables or shellfish combined with eggs and maybe cream and cheese which is baked in a pastry shell. Most of us now create our own combinations of mixtures, and the quiche has deservedly become a popular supper or luncheon dish. It is best eaten warm, after it has been baked and left out of the oven for about ten minutes. But it is also good cold, accompanied with salads, and is often a first choice in a picnic.

Quiches can be made in stages, another attraction for me. The pastry can be made days before and kept in the refrigerator. In fact shortcrust pastry can be well chilled for a few hours or several days — or even deep frozen for a couple of months. This is referred to as 'relaxing the dough' which must be reassuring to any cook. It does help the final pastry to have that crumbly melt-on-the-tongue quality which is so seductive.

There is now on the market a bewildering variety of tins and baking dishes in which to cook your quiche. The best are undoubtedly the heavy tin fluted rings with separate bottoms; these allow the quiche to be easily removed from the tin after it has been baked. Those glazed earthenware dishes decorated with recipes in a sloping script are a gimmick best avoided.

Impure as we are, there is still a distinction to be made when buying these tins. Quiche tins have a greater depth than tart or flan tins. In a 5 cm/2 inch deep quiche tin you can put a great deal more filling than in the wider but shallower tart tins. You need not add eggs to a tart mixture — you can make a filling with cream as in the mushroom tart below. Indeed, a diet-conscious cook could make a splendid tart with skimmed milk plus a filling. But once you have eaten a mouthful of pastry it seems to me you might just as well use cream after all. Possibly it is the quiches made with crab or the Lorraine with its tiny chunks of smoked bacon which seem the most tempting. But with conscious vegetarian proselytyzing I would suggest that if the pastry is seductively melting and the mixture has been made with cream and quality cheeses, both these quiches tend to be too rich. It is a more exquisite dish when the quiche is made with vegetables only. Indeed, these quiches appear to be the most common in the delicatessen shops.

Shortcrust pastry
350 g/12 oz plain sifted flour*
225 g/8 oz butter**
4 tablespoons cold water
½ teaspoon salt

These amounts are enough for two pastry cases, for either a quiche or a tart.

---

* Wholefood purists would insist on wholemeal flour of 100 per cent or less extraction. This flour makes a pastry which is heavy and somewhat brittle. It is all a matter of personal taste. If you eat pastry seldom — as I do — then I tend to make it in the classic manner above, but I also give the wholemeal version to use with the Roquefort and avocado as these are on the rich side and would be far too sickly with a classic, butter-made shortcrust.
** Wholefood purists would also object to the butter, and use margarine or a vegetable fat made especially by Mapletons called Nutter instead. But both are high in saturated fats, like butter, and they do not make pastry of the same excellence. Here again, you have to examine your own diet to see whether it is too high in diary produce or not.

Keep the butter in the coldest part of the refrigerator and grate it into the sifted flour. Mix together with your hands, so that fat and flour are amalgamated. Because the butter is grated, this only takes half a minute. Add the salt and then the water, collecting the paste into a large ball. It should have a slightly bouncy consistency, caused by the gluten becoming stretchy. Pop the whole lot in a plastic bag and keep in the refrigerator until you need it.

When the time has come to bake the pastry case, take out the dough, cut it in half and then cut a quarter off each half. This smaller piece is for the rim. (Pop the other half back in the refrigerator, if you are not making two quiches.) Butter your baking tin, place the largest piece of pastry on to the bottom tin and smear the pastry into position with fingers or the heel of your palm. Cut your smaller piece of pastry in two or three pieces and roll them into sausage shapes so that they will fit the inside rim of the tin. Smear that pastry into position. Cut a piece of foil, fill it with dried beans and bake in a preheated oven at 400°F/200°C/Gas Mark 6 for 10 to 15 minutes, or until it is just cooked through. Take out the foil and the beans. You can refrigerate for a day if you wish.

Wholemeal pastry (makes one quiche)
225 g/8 oz wholemeal flour
1 teaspoon baking powder
3 tablespoons sunflower oil
3 tablespoons cold water

Mix the flour and baking powder together, and then the oil and water. Stir the liquid in and mix quickly into a paste. Wrap the pastry ball in foil or cling film and refrigerate for an hour or a day. If the paste is too crumbly to roll out, smear it on to the cooking dish with the palm of fingers into the shape and size you want. Bake blind in a pre-heated oven 425°F/218°C/Gas Mark 7 for 10 minutes.

Spinach quiche

450 g/1 lb leaf spinach
100 g/4 oz curd cheese
100 g/4 oz double Gloucester cheese
50 g/2 oz butter
4 eggs
Pinch of nutmeg
1 cooked pastry case 5 cm/2 inch depth 20 cm/8 inch wide

Wash the spinach and shake it dry of water. Let it drain in a colander for half an hour. Then tear the leaves into smallish pieces. Melt the butter in a saucepan, put the spinach in the butter, place a lid on the pan, and let cook over a low heat for five minutes, giving it a stir only once so that you don't lose too much steam. Take from the heat and add salt, pepper, nutmeg; then the curd cheese. Add to the spinach, stirring it in, so that it melts. Beat the 4 eggs, and add those with the grated double Gloucester to the spinach mixture, before pouring it gently into the pastry case. Bake in a pre-heated oven 400°F/200°C/ Gas Mark 6 for 30 minutes.

Roquefort is wickedly expensive but as the cheese is so pungently strong and delicious, you need very little if you are going to cook with it. The quiche below requires only 170 g/6 oz and as it will easily feed six, that is not too harsh on the pocket.

Roquefort has been eaten since Roman times. It was the favourite cheese of Charlemagne. It is cured naturally in the caves of Combalou and has been protected by government charters since the thirteenth century.

It was, of course, the first authentic blue cheese. It is made from the milk of an especially handsome-looking sheep, and the cheese should have a moist buttery texture and taste rich and salty. Do not buy from a cheese that looks dry and where the blue veining is not even from the centre to the edge.

Roquefort quiche
1 cooked pastry case
170 g/6 oz roquefort cheese
75 g/3 oz curd cheese
75 g/3 oz cottage cheese
3 tablespoons yoghurt
2 egg whites
1 egg
1 bunch of spring onions
1 bunch of parsley

Chop the parsley and onions. Mix all the ingredients together in a bowl and season with a little freshly-ground pepper. Smooth the mixture over the cooked pastry case and bake in a pre-heated oven 425°F/218°C/Gas Mark 7, for 25 to 30 minutes. Allow the quiche to settle once it is out of the oven for a further five minutes before serving.

Avocado flan
1 cooked wholemeal pastry case
3 avocados, stoned and peeled
2 egg yolks
175 ml/½ pint sunflower oil
75 g/3 oz curd cheese
75 g/3 oz cottage cheese
2 crushed cloves of garlic
12 black olives

Make a mayonnaise with the egg yolks, sunflower oil and crushed garlic. Purée half of one avocado and beat this purée into the mayonnaise. Combine the curd and cottage cheeses and add about one third of the mayonnaise, spoon this mixture over the cooked pastry case. Slice the rest of the avocados and arrange them in the purée. There should be enough to fill the case. Spoon the rest of the avocado mayonnaise over the top, decorate with halves of the stoned olives and a

91

little watercress. Let the flan rest for an hour or more before serving.

Mushroom tart
450 g/1 lb mushrooms
225 g/8 oz onions
1 bunch spring onions
275 ml/¹⁄₂ pint single cream
50 g/2 oz grated parmesan
50 g/2 oz grated gruyère
50 g/2 oz butter
Salt and pepper
1 cooked 27.5 x 2.5 cm/11 x 1 inch pastry case

Slice the mushrooms and onions, place them all into a saucepan with the butter. Let them cook over a low heat for five minutes. Add salt, pepper, grated cheeses, cream and the chopped spring onions. Stir well, then spoon the mixture over the pastry case before pouring the cream over the lot. Bake as above.

Mushroom and tofu tart
Instead of the single cream use a packet of Morinaga tofu. When the mushrooms are cooked, add the tofu to the saucepan and stir the mixture, then pour it into the pastry case and bake for the same time.

PIZZA

On the evening of Christmas Day one year in the port of Naples, having only eaten bread and cheese for lunch, I dodged an appealing line of whores who could have stepped straight out of Bob Fosse's *Sweet Charity* (does Hollywood copy low life or vice versa?) and sat down ravenously to a Neapolitan pizza. I ate two.

Spring seems as good a season as any to think about them . . . Pizzas have now become a world-famous convenience food, which is perhaps why we have forgotten to cook them at home. The two I ate in Naples, the home of the pizza, reminded me of how good they can be. Originally, they must have been a quick snack which used up a piece of dough left over from bread-making. One can see how easily the dish might have been created: the dough roughly flattened on a baking sheet, some tomato purée smeared over it and a few olives strewn over that. Southern Italy's answer to bread and dripping.

The pizza proper should have a light yeasty base of a good flavour with the dough pliable and stretched thinly — so that the flour is important. Use an unbleached plain, white bread flour, not the usual household plain or self-raising flour. You can make a dough from these, of course, but it will be tasteless and the dough will not have the elasticity and liveliness of one made from bread flour. You could also make your base from a 81 per cent wholewheat flour, which would give it more flavour still, but a heavier and rather more chewy dough. Wholefood purists would possibly insist on 100 per cent wholemeal flour; the resulting flavour is one which competes with, and sometimes triumphs over, the garlic and tomato filling, while chewing the base and outside crust can take a deal of time.

I have made pizza bases from all three flours and have no preference. It comes down to the type of pizza your palate demands, to whether the pizza is a main course or a snack, and to whether you need the nutrition of a wholemeal flour.

What you put on that base is again a matter of personal choice, though do beware of strewing the top with remnants of other meals plus those olives left over from last month's party. The filling should be cooking while the dough is rising, as the flavours need time to amalgamate and the sauce to thicken.

Pizzas not only have a cooked filling smeared over the proved dough, so that the flavours are soaked up by the base, but they are then further decorated, generally with both anchovies and black olives. If you have no objection to fish, a 50 g/1¾ oz tin of anchovies is about right for a pizza this size. In this recipe I have used a mixture of black olives, capers and fresh tomatoes. A pizza needs something sharp, tangy or salty to give it that extra zest on the palate. The cooked filling uses a tin of tomatoes, because of the expense of making a pizza at this time of year wholly out of fresh tomatoes.

The early developments of the Neapolitan pizza (which then was the only one topped with cheese) was made with salted sardines (hence our use of anchovies), but the basic mixture was onions, tomatoes, garlic and black olives. Now, of course, in the local pizza bars from Salford to Sienna there are a dozen varieties of pizza to choose from. There is also a mammoth pizza, called a *calzone*, where the dough has been turned over like a giant Cornish pastie and the filling, with the addition of a couple of eggs, is inside.

The pizza recipe below is enough for four people. It is made on a 30 X 35 cm/12 X 14 inch baking tray.

Pizza dough

225 g/½ lb strong white flour or 81 per cent wholewheat or 100 per cent wholemeal.
15 g/½ oz yeast
½ teaspoon salt
2 tablespoons olive oil
2 tablespoons warm milk
1 egg
2-3 tablespoons warm water

Place the bowl with the sieved flour and salt in it somewhere warm for a few minutes. Warm the milk and add it to the yeast in a cup, stir the two together and let it begin to ferment — about 10 minutes. Add the creamed yeast to the flour, and then the egg, olive oil and two tablespoons of the warm water. Stir well. Then start to work the dough with your hands. It may or may not need the extra tablespoon of water. When the mixture has become a smooth dough, form it into a ball, place in a covered bowl and leave to rise — about two hours.

Oil a baking sheet. Take the ball of dough and smooth it down over the sheet with the sides of your hands, pressing and pulling the dough, and allowing a little more dough at the edges so that it will hold the filling. Cover with a cloth and let it rest for about 10 minutes, before adding the filling.

Pizza filling
2 medium sized onions
1 medium sized green pepper
5 crushed cloves garlic
1/2 teaspoon salt
2 tablespoons olive oil
1 teaspoon each oregano and marjoram
400 g/14 oz tin of tomatoes
2 tablespoons tomato purée
2 tablespoons of capers
5 fresh tomatoes
12 stoned black olives

Slice the pepper and the onions, fry the herbs in the olive oil for a few minutes, add the crushed garlic, stir into the oil, and then add the sliced onions, pepper and salt. Let it simmer over a low flame for 15 minutes, and then add the tin of tomatoes. Bring to the boil and allow to simmer again for 45 minutes. It should be a thick sauce now. Add the tomato purée and let it cook, without the lid of the saucepan on, for another five minutes, so that the sauce thickens and reduces a little more.

Smear this filling over the rested dough on the baking sheet, decorate with slices of fresh tomato, the capers and the stoned olives. Let the pizza rest again for another 10 minutes. Place in a pre-heated oven at 425°F/228°C/Gas Mark 7 for 15 minutes, and then turn the oven down to 375°F/190°C/Gas Mark 5 for a further 15 minutes. The filling should never dry out, so check at half time and if it looks too cooked, cover with greaseproof paper.

If you have any pizza over, it can be gently warmed up in the oven, but cover again with greaseproof paper.

AVOCADO

A ripe avocado eaten with a sauce vinaigrette that is made with lemon and a suspicion of garlic is bliss, but the flavour depends utterly on how exactly right that vinaigrette sauce is. Instead of the usual 1 to 4 ratio between the lemon and the oil, it needs a 1 to 3 ratio and for perfection I would also add a tablespoon of the thinnest shavings of spring onion.

I do wonder when avocados were discovered by the Europeans in the New World (they are first mentioned in 1526 in a report by Ovido, historian to Charles V, describing the flesh as similar to butter), whether they were eaten with salt, vinegar or in what way prepared? Possibly, as it would have been in Mexico, the Europeans first tasted avocado in a dish which has come down to us as guacamole. However, unlike other fresh discoveries — the potato, tomato, runner beans, peanuts, chocolate and vanilla — the avocado pear did not become popular.

It was largely a problem of propagation. You just don't get a good fruit from the seed, which is possibly why those spindly plants on the kitchen window sill with their frill of leaves look so dismal. It was not until the turn of the century that it was discovered avocados produce fruit of excellent quality if propagated by budding and grafting.

Now, no longer an exotic rarity, they are grown all over the world; Israel began exporting them in the late fifties and so made them plentiful. The best, fattest and quite the most sublime tasting of all the dozen or so varieties, are the large smooth-skinned green ones which originate in the West Indies. It was these I enjoyed in Australia where one the size of a charentais melon cost next to nothing.

Some years ago in one of my economical moods I surveyed three black sponge-like avocados and their withering interiors. Half of the flesh tasted foul and had to be thrown away, but the rest was only veined delicately with black and tasted good. Feeling experimental I added the flesh to some beaten eggs and scrambled the lot in butter. To my horror it turned into the perfect entrée for the Charles Addams family — the whole dish turned black. But the flavour was superb.

I hope the following recipes will not turn black, but the sliced flesh of the avocado will always do so if left exposed to the air, unless rubbed with lemon juice. However, once a dish is prepared, the purée, the soup and the guacamole can be refrigerated for a day before and the fresh green colour still remain unsullied by any mourning spots. One should, of course, be careful about buying the avocados in the first place, choosing ones uniform in colour without cracks, bruises or those dark sunken splodges. Hard avocados will ripen in a few days at room temperature.

Avocado purée I

3 ripe avocados
Zest and juice from 1 lemon
1 clove of garlic, crushed
140 ml/¼ pint of olive oil or natural yoghurt
Salt and pepper
5 spring onions (optional)

Scrape the zest from the lemon peel, squeeze the juice from the lemon, crush the garlic and extract all the flesh from the avocado, especially the very bright green flesh that adheres closely to the skin. Put it all into the blender with the seasoning and add the olive oil quite slowly until it has turned into a thick cream. If using yoghurt, there is no need to add it slowly. The avocado flesh can be added to the yoghurt in the blender. Made with yoghurt the purée is more refreshing. This will happen quite quickly. Serve with

97

the spring onions chopped very finely sprinkled over the top. It can be eaten with toast, spread on pancakes, used like a mayonnaise with crudités, or in a chilled soup. The above quantities will make enough for 12.

Cold avocado soup I

2 ripe avocados
1 pint of vegetable stock
275 ml/½ pint of skimmed milk
1 packet Morinaga tofu
Salt and pepper
Chopped parsley, mint or chives

It is well worth taking the trouble to make your own stock for the soup. A vegetarian stock cube tastes much the same as a chicken stock cube — whether it has MSG in it or not it still tastes of monosodium glutamate, turning home-made soup into something reminiscent of a tin or a packet.

I find the most useful vegetable stock can be made from onion and celery stalks, chopped, boiled, blended, then sieved. A bay leaf, parsley stalks, outside leaves of lettuce and cabbage can all be used, their flavour extracted and then bottled and kept in the refrigerator. There is another factor in this recipe too, all chilled soups somehow make the taste of the stock cube more apparent. So if you cannot be bothered to make a stock, omit it altogether.

Scoop out all the flesh from the avocados, place into the blender and add the milk and stock until the flesh has completely disintegrated. Then add the tofu and season by tasting. Sprinkle the chopped herbs over the surface of the soup.

Cold avocado soup II

2 ripe avocados
1 clove garlic
1 teaspoon lemon juice

pinch of sea salt
$1/2$ teaspoon tabasco sauce
2 tablespoons yoghurt
875 ml/$1^1/_2$ pints skimmed milk

Scoop out the flesh from the avocados and place into a blender. Add the crushed garlic, lemon juice, sea salt, yoghurt and skimmed milk. Blend together to the consistency of a thin sauce. Chill in the refrigerator for an hour. Remember cold intensifies the saltiness of a food. Bring the soup out of the refrigerator 15 minutes before serving.

Guacamole

2 avocados
2 tomatoes
1 onion
1 green pepper
1 green chilli
Several sprigs of coriander
Salt and pepper
1 tablespoon lemon juice

Peel the tomatoes, chop the onion, pepper and chilli very fine with the tomato, add the lemon juice and season. Cut the avocados, remove the stones, scrape out all the flesh and mash it up well. Add to the first mixture and pile it in to the avocado skins. Decorate with the chopped coriander and think of Cortes.

Summer

In northern Europe we value the summer more; suddenly the abundance of vegetables and fruit is upon us. By middle to late June there seems to be a cornucopia of garden produce to choose from. It is the most exciting and satisfying time of the year. Most of the herbs are about to flower. There are peas, mange-touts, broad beans, spinach, asparagus, different varieties of lettuce, new potatoes.

It is a time for light dishes, soufflés, mousses, tians, timbales and roulades. It is also a time when the salads continue, but because we have a greater choice of vegetables we can now be more adventurous. Almost any vegetable that we eat cooked and hot can also be enjoyed as a salad, suitably sliced and dressed, either raw or lightly cooked *al dente*. For a start try eating raw asparagus; its flavour is more pronounced, and it does not require melted butter.

Green beans when young, whether broad, French or runner, can all be eaten raw. Nothing is more delicious than a huge platter of crudités in the summer months with the vegetables freshly picked, their colours radiant and burnished, with a huge bowl of aioli mayonnaise. (Add 2 crushed cloves of raw garlic to the finished mayonnaise). It amazes me that people always extol the lavish cold tables at restaurants and hotels, that they find a range of salads always tempting, that even the reputation of an establishment can be made with the splendour of its hors d'oeuvres, but at home the salads are dull, using the same ingredients, lettuce, tomato and cucumber.

Imaginative salads need a little planning and some time spent in preparation, but they are the easiest foods for entertaining, they never fail to please and delight guests and the combinations of vegetables, flavourings and dressings are well-nigh infinite.

There is no end to recipes for iced soups, nor for fruit soups, or fruit and vegetables soups. They are particularly good and refreshing if the summer ever settles down into a heat wave. Some of the nicest are the simplest to make.

Cucumber and grapefruit soup
1 large cucumber
The juice from 2 grapefruits
275 ml/½ pint low fat yoghurt
Fresh chopped mint

Grate the cucumber, skin and all, blend in a liquidizer with the grapefruit juice and yoghurt. Taste and season. Garnish after cooling it in the refrigerator with the chopped mint. You could also add a glass of dry sherry or dry white wine to this soup, as you could with a cucumber and apple soup, made as above but adding the flesh from two cooking apples after they have been steamed and puréed. Fennel and orange soup with a dash of pernod or ouzo is also good.

RUNNER BEANS

Runner beans which we English grow in every back garden in the summer get short shrift in our cooking. They are always thinly sliced and boiled. Their flavour is excellent (I cannot think why the French dismiss them) and they deserve other ways of cooking and serving.

Runner beans with tomato and garlic

450 g/1 lb runner beans
4 or 5 tomatoes
3 crushed cloves of garlic
1 tablespoon olive oil

Top and tail and pare the string off the sides of the beans, chop them in to 2.5 cm/1 inch lengths and cook them in a little boiling water until just tender (about 4 minutes). Drain them. Pour the olive oil into the pan and add the chopped tomatoes and garlic. Let them cook for a few minutes, or until the tomatoes have just begun to purée themselves and make a sauce, then add the cooked beans. Stir well, so that the beans are covered in the sauce, and serve.

MIXED VEG

Vegetable markets tend to fascinate most of us, but I fear the English markets are often a let-down. They disguise inferior produce, or sell at a minor discount a heap of discoloured vegetables that other nationalities would have thrown away. It is partly our tradition as meat-eaters of awesome capacity, respecting the roast, while boiling the vegetables into a sodden sponge. It is only to be expected that we have no national vegetable dishes, except for cauliflower cheese. Our climate is partly to blame, too, for it makes all the summer vegetables far more expensive than in the Mediterranean countries.

But markets abroad absorb my senses. The aubergines, peppers and courgettes are as glossily burnished as if fashioned in wax. Each spinach leaf and each head of lettuce seems sculpted: the herbs form the most heady pot-pourri and those giant marmande tomatoes and roped pearly white garlics are for me, unashamedly, objects of sensual desire.

The next two recipes here make the most of all the vegetables and herbs which are in profusion in the summer months. They are recipes not usually thought of as vegetarian fare and the ratatouille must be the most common foreign dish ever made. Yet the pipérade, which is in some ways similar, is not so well known. Nevertheless it is an easy dish to make and people unfamiliar with it are seduced immediately into becoming addicts.

These recipes differ from most usual ones in that there is a preliminary cooking of the tomatoes with their skin and green stalks, which ensures the essential intensity of tomato flavour. The aroma of a tomato plant is something we all inhale with delight and it derives from the leaves and stalk. The tomato flavour that we miss we have quite often thrown away with the skins. The marmande tomato is of course the tomato *par excellence*, and the largest. If not eaten raw, it should be stuffed with garlic, herbs, local grated cheese and a few breadcrumbs to bind the mixture, then grilled.

Ratatouille Nicoise

2 *large aubergines*
3 *large onions*
6 *small peppers*
3 *large tomatoes*
5 *cloves crushed garlic*
3 *tablespoons olive oil*
Seasoning

Cut the unpeeled aubergines into $\frac{1}{2}$cm/$\frac{1}{4}$ inch slices: sprinkle a little salt on each one and leave to drain for up to two hours. Wash the slices under a running tap and pat them dry. Slice onions and peppers, cube the aubergines and cook in the olive oil for about 30 minutes. Cook the tomatoes as in the above recipe and add the purée. Cook for another 20 minutes until all the vegetables are quite soft. Taste for seasoning. This is best kept for a day before it is eaten. Any fresh herbs like oregano, basil or coriander leaves can be added before serving.

How we make ratatouille and what we exactly put into it is very much a personal choice. Some people like to have the vegetables less cooked than I do, so that they are separate and distinguishable. I prefer all flavours blended into one. Other people find olive oil too rich and prefer to use sunflower oil — others would not put as much garlic into the dish as I do. And certainly most recipes insist on courgettes being added as well. That is a matter which I am easy about, but if you add them they must be treated like aubergines: sliced, salted and left for a couple of hours, so that they lose some of their water content.

Pipérade
6 small green peppers
6 small onions
5 cloves of crushed garlic
500 g / 1 lb tomatoes
6 eggs
3 tablespoons olive oil

Cook tomatoes with skins and stalks in a tablespoon of oil with a pinch of salt in a closed saucepan over a low heat until soft — about five minutes. Put through a sieve and reserve. Slice peppers, onions and crush garlic; cook in a shallow, thick-bottomed pan in the rest of the oil, so that it gently bubbles. But watch that it does not stick. Give the occasional stir. When the peppers are soft (about 30 minutes) pour in the tomato purée and cook for another five minutes. Taste for seasoning. Beat the eggs in a bowl and pour into the pan, raise the heat and cook as if for scrambled eggs — that is stir and beat with a fork until the eggs are just cooked. They will collect all the juices, so the mixture should be just congealed.

PURÉES

Purées which we can spread on biscuits or toast, or pile into croûtes, stuff into celery stalks, tomatoes and eggs can be the most delicious first courses or appetizers that exist. They can all be prepared a day or two before they are eaten. They keep well, covered in a refrigerator. But we may be a little narrow in our choice of what is puréed and how we flavour it.

We know hummus from Greece but I do not believe that any hummus we have had here in a restaurant is as good as the one we can make at home. I always feel astonished that such an uninspired object as a chick pea can turn into a paste which is so delicate and earthy at the same time. There is no need to soak chick peas, though soaking never does any harm, but they will need a greater quantity of cooking water. When cooked, they more than double their bulk. Chick peas need a good two to three hours' boiling. In a pressure cooker they take only half an hour. They do not disintegrate like other dried beans when cooked; so test with the point of a knife and if the pea breaks open it is done. As with all pulses, add salt after they are cooked. The harder you blend, the creamier the colour and consistency. Hummus made at home should end up looking a little like clotted cream.

One of the most beautiful purées is made from flageolets. It is the most highly prized dried bean in France and deservedly so. This type of haricot is picked young; so it is the most tender of all the pulses. It too does not need soaking. When storing flageolets use a smoked glass or opaque container, as they will quickly lose their delicate colour.

Any of the dried pulses, with added spices or herbs, can make the most delicious purées. Try boiling the beans with lemon skins, bay leaves or sprigs of rosemary. Then, after the beans are tender, add sea salt, freshly-ground pepper, garlic, olive oil and the juice from a lemon. Then experiment with various herbs and spices, tasting the purée as you blend it in the liquidizer.

If you are fortunate enough to have a herb garden, or even a small window with a few essential herbs in it, the time to pick them is before they flower. This is one of the great advantages of being free from the imprisonment of thinking you must eat meat; once it is erased from the diet, indeed from the mind altogether, you are ready to experiment and try a vast new range of flavours and combine them in original ways.

Aubergines lend themselves beautifully to being puréed. It is my opinion that they show their best qualities in that way. They also combine well with purées of mushroom, olive, carrot and hot radish. You can bake aubergines at the bottom of the oven while cooking something else, turn the oven off and leave overnight. Or they can be baked in a pre-heated oven at a medium heat for an hour. Place them on an oiled baking tray. When cooked, pierce the skin, peel it away and scoop out the flesh. Sometimes the seeds are not as tender as the rest. If so, discard them.

Hummus
170 g/6 oz chick peas
Juice from one lemon
Generous handful of chopped mint
3 crushed cloves of garlic
140 ml/¼ pint olive oil
Sea salt and freshly-ground pepper

Place the cooked chick peas in the blender with about 140 ml/¼ pint of the liquid it has cooked in. Add the lemon juice, garlic, mint and seasoning. Blend so that the peas disintegrate, then add the olive oil in a steady stream. Liquidize for up to two minutes, or until the mixture has turned deep cream in colour and is quite smooth.

Purée de flageolets
200 g/7 oz dried flageolets
1 teaspoon dill weed, or 2 teaspoons fresh marjoram or lovage or basil
2 tablespoons olive oil

2 tablespoons double cream
Seasoning

Boil the flageolets in 3 litres/3 quarts of water for about an hour, but have a peep at them at the end of cooking, because they tend suddenly to soak up the liquid.

Drain the beans and put them in the liquidizer with the olive oil, the herb and seasoning, blend, then add the cream and blend again. You will have a thick, pale green purée, spread it on wholemeal toast or eat it with crudités.

Indian aubergine purée
2 large aubergines
1 chopped onion
Handful of chopped coriander leaves
1 teaspoon garam masala
1 finely chopped green chilli, or ½ teaspoon chilli powder
Juice from 1 lemon
1 tablespoon each yoghurt and sour cream
1 tablespoon roasted sesame seeds

Scoop the cooked flesh from the baked aubergines, add all the other ingredients except for the sesame seeds and blend well. Before serving, sprinkle the sesame seeds over the purée.

TOMATOES

Every year I search for the quintessence of tomato. Ailsa Craig, marmande, Roma and Gardener's Delight all do well in an unheated greenhouse. The first three often taste disappointingly bland, though the marmande and the Roma cook well. Gardener's Delight has a good sharp flavour, but tiny fruit. Why is it then that both marmande and Roma tomatoes on the Continent taste strongly of tomato? Is it the soil, is it the manure, is it the seed itself?

Or is it that tomatoes need baking hot sun for their flavour to be pronounced?

There are countless tomato recipes which always tell you to peel and deseed the tomatoes. I have never deseeded a tomato in my life. Nor do I understand why recipes instruct you to perform this thankless chore. In the following soup recipes, the tomatoes are sieved and in the omelette recipe the peel gives flavour and the seeds pattern the eggs pleasantly.

It is traditional to make chutney with malt vinegar. I loathe the pungent smell of malt vinegar and dislike its harsh flavour. Cider vinegar is more expensive, but one can then taste the other ingredients in the chutney. Is it necessary for chutney always to be a dark brown mush? Is it necessary for it to be cooked with vast amounts of sugar? I don't think so. The vinegar is the preservative.

You may well consider the amount of garlic in the chutney is madness, but its flavour changes radically in the cooking. If your fear of garlic amounts to a mild paranoia, use shallots. If you cannot get your hands on shallots, use pickling onions.

Nearly five years ago now I began making both soup and sauces from fresh tomatoes using the skins and the green stalks. They are so immensely superior to any soup or sauce made from tinned tomatoes or from fresh without using the skin and stalks, that I have become obsessive in preaching its worth.

Here is my tomato soup:

Tomato soup I
900 g/2 lb tomatoes
1 glass dry sherry
1½ pints water
Pinch of salt
Pepper (optional)
Couple of cloves of garlic (optional)

Make sure that as many tomatoes as possible have

their green stalks on. Pierce each one with a knife so that when the heat starts the juices will run easily, place them into a saucepan and add the pinch of salt and glass of sherry. Put the lid on the saucepan and place over a low heat and forget about them for five minutes. When they are cool put everything through a sieve, or you can liquidize them first and then sieve them. You could also before cooking add a couple of cloves of garlic and a few turns of the pepper mill.

I have tried making this sauce with the imported Dutch tomatoes that we have in the winter and even they have flavour. A true discovery, as I had rejected them for years; but obviously the flavour was all in the skin, which I had peeled and thrown away.

For a sauce I would put this soup back on to the stove and reduce by a third.

Tomato soup II
800 g/1 lb 12 oz tomatoes
1100 ml/2 pints water
5 basil leaves
2 crushed cloves of garlic
1 glass dry sherry
1 tablespoon olive oil
1 teaspoon lemon juice
Seasoning

Simmer the tomatoes with their skins and stalks in the sherry over a low heat with a pinch of salt and the crushed garlic cloves for about 5 minutes, or until they are soft. Add the water and bring to the boil. Allow to cool and blend, then sieve. Discard bits of stalk, skin and pips. Chop the basil leaves finely and add them to the oil and lemon immediately to ensure they do not blacken. Reheat the soup and serve, adding the basil sauce to each individual soup bowl.

Tomato and basil omelette
6 eggs
325 g/11 oz tomatoes
25 g/1 oz butter
1 tablespoon olive oil
5 basil leaves
2 tablespoons single cream
Seasoning

Melt the butter and oil in a pan. Chop the tomatoes coarsely, and fry them for a minute or two. Add the beaten eggs, and allow the underneath to cook. Chop the basil leaves, mix with the cream pour this over the top of the omelette, and then place pan under a hot grill, so that the top is cooked through.

Green tomato chutney
1 kg/2 lb 4 oz green tomatoes
23 large cloves of garlic, or 2 heads of smaller garlic
550 ml/1 pint apple cider vinegar
3 chopped green chillies
100 g/4 oz root ginger
1 tablespoon brown sugar
1 teaspoon salt

Chop the tomatoes, coarsely, peel the garlic cloves by pouring boiling water on them, and leave for a few minutes. The skins will then slip off with ease. Chop chillies and peel and slice the ginger thinly. Place all ingredients into a preserving pan with the sugar, salt and half the amount of wine vinegar. Bring to the boil and simmer, stirring the mixture until the tomatoes and garlic are cooked through — about 20 minutes. Then add the rest of the vinegar*, bring to the boil again and simmer until the chutney begins to thicken a little. Leave to cool and then bottle. Can be eaten

* If the tomatoes have made a lot of liquid they may not need the rest of the wine vinegar.

after five months. Perfect for brightening those February blues.

BROAD BEANS

We import broad beans from Cyprus from early spring to tide us over to our first crop here. When young they can be eaten whole, pod and all, boiled for five minutes in a little salted water then tossed briefly in butter. They are strongly distinct in flavour and their history, as Mrs Beeton says, goes back to 'time immemorial'.

It is often quoted that Pythagoras informed his disciples to stay away from beans. This is not, as commonly thought, the master's anxiety that his pupils might foul the air with flatulent contagion, but possibly refers to the fact that the broad bean when dried makes an excellent counter for political elections and that Pythagoras wished his disciples to abstain from voting.

In Mediterranean countries in the winter you can still see the bulging sacks of gigantic broad beans. They are beige and dun-coloured, hard as walnut shells and need overnight soaking and slow cooking to release their earthly bouquet.

The broad bean season in England is short, a mere six weeks, unless you have your own garden and stagger the showings. It is worth exploring other ways of cooking and enjoying this vegetable than merely boiling the beans and throwing away the pods (a heretical act, in my opinion; I use the pods to make a soup or a purée). But let me stress that if you buy the broad bean young, then it will need only topping and tailing before cooking, when the whole vegetable is eaten.

To begin with, you can always choose to eat the beans raw, as part of a dish of crudités with an aioli mayonnaise. Nothing is more refreshing than a great platter of sliced seasonal vegetables with a couple of accompanying sauces to begin a meal. Raw broad beans I associate with Greece, uneven wooden tables wobbling on the quayside piled with beans while the fishermen shell them in between knocking back the ouzos, eating the bean as a *meze* and, alas, throwing the pods into the sea.

In France, the herb summer savory is traditionally cooked with the beans. In fact Thompson and Morgan in their seed catalogues suggest you grow the herb with the plants as a protection against black fly. Elizabeth David warns against the bitterness if you cook the herb, and as savory is undeniably strong it would be circumspect to chop only a few leaves and add it to the butter or the cream the cooked beans are tossed in.

If you have a large amount of broad beans and don't want to bother to dry them and keep them over the winter, you can boil them until soft then blend or mince them so that you have a *dry crumbly purée*, which will be high in protein, vitamins and carbohydrate. This can be deep frozen and used for the soup, the purée, or the falafels and faiscedda below. It is one way of enjoying the broad bean out of season.

Broad bean soup
450 g/1 lb beans in their pods
25 g/1 oz butter
140 ml/¼ pint of single cream
Seasoning

Pod the beans, then boil the pods for 15 minutes in a little salted water. Cook the beans separately in the butter and a little more water until they are soft. Save everything, but be careful that you have not over-salted the water the vegetables boil in. If doubtful, it is best to add the salt at the last stage of cooking when one can judge it exactly.

Place pods and their water into the blender and turn on at top speed so that everything disintegrates into a deepwater bottle-green haze. Then sieve the mixture and throw away all the shreds and hairs from the pods. Now blend the beans in the butter and water, but you don't have to sieve this lot unless the beans are very old and have that tough outer skin. Combine the two stocks, reheat gradually adding the single cream at the last minute and taste again for seasoning.

Purée de fèves
Again use 450 g/1 lb broad beans, pods as well. Cook them as for the soup above, but drain off the liquid and reserve for stock. Blend the pods and sieve them. Put that thin purée back into the blender and add the cooked beans, 25 g/1 oz softened butter, 1 tablespoon of thick cream, salt and pepper. Blend all together and serve at room temperature.

Broad beans cooked in stock
450 g/1 lb broad beans, podded
Vegetable stock, made from garlic, onions and celery
25 g/1 oz butter
2 egg yolks
Juice of 1 lemon

Just cover the podded beans with the stock and butter. Let it boil without the lid on the saucepan so that the stock reduces, but watch the pan so that the beans don't dry out and burn.

When the beans are tender (their age determines how long they boil, but you should have about 3 tablespoons of stock left), pour the stock into a bowl containing the egg yolks and lemon juice. Mix these together well and return them to the pan, cooking gently without boiling until the sauce begins to thicken. Pour it over the beans and serve.

Broad beans with tomato and garlic

225 g/½ lb tomatoes
1 tablespoon dry sherry
5 cloves of crushed garlic
450 g/1 lb broad beans
Seasoning

Cook the tomatoes in their skins in a covered pan with the sherry and crushed garlic. Boil the beans separately. Sieve the tomatoes after about 10 minutes when they have already disintegrated into a mush. Drain the beans and serve them with the tomato and garlic sauce.

Falafels

In Israel these are made from chick peas, in Egypt (where they are called talamia) they are made from whole broad beans. They are delicious as an appetizer or can be served as a first course with a platter of crudités. They are best eaten warm, if made out of chick peas, it is best to use either a little yeast or baking powder. This recipe uses the broad bean dry purée (see page 112).

350 g/¾ lb dry broad bean purée
2 onions, finely chopped
2 cloves crushed garlic
1 tablespoon summer savory, chopped
1 egg
Salt and black pepper
Olive oil
Butter
Flour

Add to the purée the onions, garlic and summer savory. Stir well then add the egg and a little salt and black pepper. Make small cakes the size of walnuts. If the mixture is too sticky to mould, then roll in flour. Shallow fry in olive oil and butter for a moment or two until brown and crisp on the outside.

Faiscedda

225 g / ½ lb dry broad bean purée (page 112)
2 tablespoons breadcrumbs
Pinch of nutmeg
2 eggs
Oil
Butter

They make this dish in Sardinia from the fresh broad beans which are plentiful there from February to March. Add to the dry purée, the breadcrumbs, nutmeg and eggs. Make a flat cake and cook it in a frying pan in oil and butter, turning it over once so that both sides are crisp and a little brown. Eat while still warm.

TIMBALES AND TIANS

In the past timbales were infrequently cooked; it was a rejected dish and it is only since the fashionable interest in nouveau cuisine that they have made a quiet reappearance. They are worthy of interest and if cooked in a mould (I use a *kugelhopf* and the accompanying sauce goes into the middle hole) they look stunning served at the table.

The traditional dish used, itself called a timbale, is an oval dish with fluted sides, but timbales can be made in soufflé dishes of all sizes, and even individual ramekins.

A timbale is a flavoured egg custard, steamed in the oven; some cooks whip the egg whites which turns it into a steamed soufflé. I prefer not to do this, as I like my timbale to be fairly substantial.

I have flavoured timbales with purées of spinach, asparagus, artichokes, cauliflower, leeks, mushrooms and onions. They can be served with a sauce, or if you eat the timbale cold, a mayonnaise — this is gourmand's delight. A timbale impresses the guests, for it looks difficult to create, yet it would be difficult to have a disaster with one, so effortlessly simple are they to make. Besides, they are definitely *haute*.

Spinach timbale

5 eggs
25 g/1 oz finely chopped onion
25 g/1 oz butter
50 g/2 oz breadcrumbs
3 tablespoons spinach purée
50 g/2 oz grated mild cheese
Pinch of nutmeg
Seasoning
275 ml/½ pint skimmed milk

Butter the mould or soufflé dish and sprinkle the bottom and sides with the breadcrumbs. Pre-heat oven to a medium heat 350°F/180°C/Gas Mark 4.

Cook the onion in the butter until it is soft, then put it into a mixing bowl with the spinach, cheese, nutmeg, seasoning, and the rest of the breadcrumbs. Beat the eggs into this mixture, then add the milk. Carefully pour the custard into the dish so as not to disturb the breadcrumbs sticking to the sides. Stand the dish in a baking tin of boiling water and let it cook in the oven for 45 minutes. The custard is done when a knife inserted in the middle comes out clean. Let the custard settle for 5 minutes after taking it out of the oven, then invert the dish over a warm platter and it should slide out quite easily.

Tians, on the other hand, must be bourgeois, for they are economic, simple and quick to create, excellent for supper or a light luncheon or good for a picnic. A tian is first of all a round or oval earthenware shallow dish which has been used, especially in the Mediterranean countries, for thousands of years. It is perfect for the gentle cooking that some vegetables demand, and if I had no other utensil, not even one saucepan, I could still eat well just using the tians. The smooth concave shape of the earthenware takes and holds the heat equally; the dish can be brought to the table and the food will still keep hot. (Timbale and tian dishes of

116

all sizes can be bought at the Elizabeth David Shop, 46 Bourne Street, London, SW1.)

I have named this dish after the tian in which it is made because it is not a quiche, having no pastry shell, nor is it a gratin, having more eggs, cheese or cream than vegetables. Omitting the pastry saves time and calories, if the earthenware is well buttered the tian will make its own base and, eaten warm as it should be — like a quiche — it will slice in portions without falling to bits. I used to think that it required a light roux base, but this too I have now omitted.

A tian should never be dry or stodgy, it ought to be light but above all else it must be moist. To ensure this use a vegetable with a high water content like tomatoes, spinach, or mushrooms and also use cream or curd cheese or tofu or yoghurt or sour cream and lastly take care that the tian is brought from the oven the moment it is cooked through. Five more minutes in the heat and it will have dried out.

The choice of what you add to the basic egg, cream, cheese mixture seems well nigh infinite and it is also, just between ourselves, highly useful for rejuvenating leftovers. If you cannot face that bowl of ratatouille one more day, here is the answer. Any vegetable purée or sauce will adapt itself happily to this treatment. Hence, if you are like me and go through life in a state of high anxiety over wasted food, this can solve some problems.

Leek tian
450 g/1 lb leeks
25 g/1 oz butter
275 ml/½ pint single cream or 1 packet Morinaga tofu
4 beaten eggs
100 g/4 oz cheddar cheese, grated
Seasoning

Wash and chop the leeks, then sauté them in a closed pan in the butter for 5 or 6 minutes, or until they are just soft but still in individual pieces. Butter the tian dish, then press the grated cheese on to the base so that it forms a layer, add the leeks, eggs, and lastly the cream or tofu and seasoning. Place in a pre-heated oven at a medium heat for 30 to 40 minutes before slicing.

In our only too few and all too often damp and grey summer months there is, to cheer us up, a huge range of fresh vegetables. Even if the rains of summer have turned the vegetable patch into the Battle of the Somme, the produce will probably taste all the better for it.

In these short summer months, with a great variety of vegetables to choose from, it is time to compete with the meat eaters and their moulded pâtés and terrines. A layered mousse or terrine (the nomenclature is highly confused and I bet EEC regulations will not be able to clarify them in a hundred years) looks highly impressive, but only too often tempts the palate with a promise which on the first nibble is a great let down.

Aesthetically the meat and poultry terrines have a limited range of colour and hue, going from raw umber to all shades of mahogany to ivory and off-white; while the vegetarians have the colours of the rainbow to play with, a veritable palette of impressionist tints to compose with in the small confines of their baking tin, a first course which could well be exhibited in the Summer Show at the Royal Academy.

Here I might warn painters and others with sensitive eyesight that fresh peas, when puréed, turn a most strident bright green, the kind of shade that Oscar Wilde complained our English grass had. Hence, this ingredient, delicious in flavour, must be used with care. I put mine, throwing caution to the winds, on top of the terrine, though I temper the viridian glow with some sorrel leaves.

All this colour concern is not complete nonsense. If you can imagine a meal that was composed of food drained of all colour, so that it was shades of white, our appetite would

118

remain unstimulated. We tend to think of such meals as invalid fare.

Just as many of us have thought of vegetarian food as fodder for cranks. But those times are past, and to prove it we have the example of nouvelle cuisine which now creates the most delectable and delicious of vegetable terrines from a variety of purées.

The only drawback that I have noticed in making these terrines is that one tends to use a lot of bowls and utensils and so it is a bit heavy on the washing up. The recipe below is for a terrine that is extremely light and for it to work you must ensure that all excess moisture is eliminated from the purées before the egg which binds them together is added.

There would be no anxieties if you added a tablespoon of double cream to a purée, or 50 g/2 oz of grated cheddar or even a light roux. But I wanted to make a terrine as light as possible and which was supremely the vegetables themselves.

I wanted the taste of summer on the plate even if it wasn't in the weather.

Enjoy the terrine with a crisp lettuce and one of the cold sauces given below.

Green terrine
1 medium cauliflower
450 g/1 lb spinach
450 g/1 lb broad beans
450 g/1 lb peas
Handful of sorrel leaves or extra spinach leaves
4 eggs
Seasoning

Slice the flowerets from the stalk of the cauliflower and then slice the stalk thinly, boil until tender and drain with care. Pop all the vegetable pieces into the blender; liquidize. However carefully you have drained the cauliflower it will still have plenty of water in it, so this is the most liquid of all the purées. Place into a bowl to cool.

Wash the spinach and squeeze extra water out of the leaves with your hands. Put into an empty saucepan over a low heat and stir with a wooden spoon until the spinach is a third of its bulk. Leave to cook then squeeze the cooked spinach again with your hands to rid it of its liquid.

Blend to a purée, and if it is so dry the liquidizer refuses to turn, then add one of the eggs to help it on its way.

Cook the broad beans and peas separately, strain the water from them and blend into purées.

You will now have four separate purées. Add one beaten egg to each purée and taste for seasoning, add a few grinds of black pepper and some sea salt where you think necessary.

Butter a terrine dish and cut out the central stalks from either the sorrel or the spinach leaves. Lay them raw on the bottom of the dish and up the sides. Place about 1 cm/½ inch cauliflower purée in the bottom, then another raw leaf of sorrel or spinach, then the spinach purée — a lovely bottle-green colour — then the pea purée, then the cauliflower and the broad bean purée, and so on, alternating white and green or dark green with light green, dividing the layers with the leaves and pressing down each layer firmly.

Put the lid of the terrine dish on if it has one. If not, cover with foil and place into a baking tin of boiling water in a pre-heated oven at 400°F/200°C/Gas Mark 6 for 30 minutes. Leave to cool and refrigerate for a few hours to a day.

To turn out, dip the outside of the terrine dish in hot water for a minute and then upturn it over a platter.

The sorrel or spinach leaves will have shrunk and made their own pattern against the green and white stripes of the terrine. It is plain fare but of such goodness. Added pleasure and decoration can be achieved by a few spoonfuls of either pistachio nuts or capers being added to the cauliflower purée.

If you have any of the purées over you can make parcels out of them by wrapping the sorrel or spinach leaves around them. They will bake in the oven, then they can be left to cool, sliced and eaten as a *meze* or appetizer.

Onion and lemon sauce

2 large onions
50 g/2 oz butter
1 lemon
Seasoning

Slice onions thinly, take the zest from the lemon and cook both in the butter in a closed saucepan for ten minutes or until the onions are soft and transparent. Leave to cool. Liquidize with the lemon juice to a purée and add the seasoning to taste. An effortless sauce to make which uses no flour and no cream but tastes heavenly.

Watercress and egg sauce

2 cooked egg yolks
1 raw egg yolk
1 lemon
Handful of watercress
275 ml/½ pint single cream or 1 packet Morinaga tofu.

Thoroughly mix the two cooked egg yolks, the raw yolk, the zest from the lemon peel, and the lemon juice together. Finely chop a generous handful of watercress and add to the egg and lemon mixture. Add the cream or tofu slowly, beating it in.

Autumn

Many of our autumn meals can be based on the soybean and its products (see pages 43-59). I hope I have managed to introduce both miso and tofu to a wider public and to have made people aware of what is a natural soy sauce. All these products have been eaten in the Far East by the majority for countless centuries when meat has been unobtainable or too expensive and fish was scarce. They are high in protein foods.

There is another soybean product which I have not included because it is almost unobtainable here, though it is popular in the States. This is tempeh (pronounced tempay). Tempeh is cooked soybeans bound together in a mass by a mycelium. It has been fermented: the same process by which we make cheese and yoghurt. It has a strong flavour, reminiscent of a mature cheddar mixed with field mushrooms. It is 19.5 per cent protein, (chicken is 21 per cent and beef is 20 per cent). The East West Centre at 196 Old Street, London EC1, makes it. And it can also be bought at the Sunwheel shop next door. I mention it here to encourage more home industries in the production of tempeh. (*The Book of Tempeh* by William Shurtleff and Akiko Aoyago published by Harper, tells all.)

Field mushrooms and fungi (pages 140-142) are possibly some of the best foods of autumn. But there is also pumpkin, a wondrous fruit with a velvety orange flesh, which makes the nicest soup in the world. It can also be diced and sautéed in olive oil with garlic and eaten as a vegetable. It can be chopped and added with other vegetables in bean stews and mixed vegetable soups. The soup is simplicity itself to make.

Pumpkin soup
900 g/2 lb pumpkin flesh
3 tablespoons olive oil
1100 ml/2 pints vegetable stock, or water
Salt and pepper

Dice the pumpkin flesh small, fry the pieces in the olive oil (you need good dark green oil with flavour). When soft, cover with the boiling vegetable stock or water and simmer for 15 minutes. Liquidize the lot and add a little sea salt and black pepper to taste.

There is also the vegetable marrow, that object much loved by the British, which is allowed to grow too large, so that it is all fibre and no taste. But they are good when no longer than 40 cm/16 inches and can be stuffed with any mixture of breadcrumbs, herbs, onion and cheese, and then baked in the oven. As a child I can recall eating marrow boiled in rings and served on stale bread to soak up the water. A disgusting dish. It was sometimes covered in white sauce. Because of this memory, I never boil marrow at all, preferring to cube the flesh and to stir-fry it with garlic and onion. The cubed flesh should still be a little firm.

Autumn is the season for pickling. Use cider vinegar whenever possible, for malt is far too astringent and pervades. Also be imaginative with the spices and herbs and there is of course no need to add large amounts of sugar to either pickles or chutney (see page 110 for Tomato chutney). The quantities given in most recipes are horrifying.

This is also the time for English celery, the only celery that tastes intrinsically of celery, but people are often put off by the soil that clings to it. It only needs a good hard scrub with a brush. It is sometimes too fibrous to be eaten au naturel with cheese, but it then makes excellent soup. Wash it, boil it, liquidize it and sieve it; add yoghurt, a little butter, sour cream, crushed garlic and a good turn of the pepper mill.

AUBERGINES

I must say that now and then I find there is something uninspiring about aubergines. They look magnificent as aesthetic objects, as if posing for illustrations on the jackets of cookery books, but to eat? That densely packed flesh like fawn blotting paper fills me with misgivings, until I recall the many excellent purées that can be made from these unpromising beginnings. And once I taste them again I am always struck anew at how drastically their character changes when they are cooked; from being obdurate, flavourless, and stodgy they become as light as a soufflé and as savoury as a wild mushroom.

Aubergines are said to have originated in India and China and gone from there to the Middle East whence many recipes have come down to us. The Italians began to grow them in the Middle Ages but they need a hot climate and a long growing season in the year, for they are annuals belonging to the nightshade family which, among other plants includes both potatoes and petunias. (Tomatoes also belong to the same genus, and I believe this is the reason why macrobiotic cooking bans all three vegetables: they share a parent that is highly toxic.) We in England managed to ignore their existence until after the Second World War when package tours and Elizabeth David simultaneously became popular. We have imported them ever since and autumn, when there is a glut of them in the Mediterranean and they should be cheaper to buy here, is the time to experiment with ways of cooking them, other than as just one of the ingredients in a ratatouille.

If the aubergines are between 15 and 30 cm/6 and 12 inches long, they are large enough to be skinned and deseeded, but size does not affect the flavour. Of the delicious purées to be enjoyed as an hors d'oeuvres, the most famous is melitzana, which is the Greek name for the same mixture which occurs in every Middle Eastern country. For this and the other purées, bake the whole aubergines in a moderate oven for about an hour (on the grill, like jacket potatoes), test with a skewer, and when they are soft or give to the touch, they are done.

Baking them rids them of their high water content, which is the main problem when cooking them in any other way. It is best always to slice the aubergines in ½ cm/¼ inch slices, sprinkle salt on them, and leave them for an hour, then rinse salt and water from the slices under a cold tap and dry with a towel. If you sidestep this process you will find that the aubergine slices soak up a vast amount of oil and are stodgy and, I think, inedible. Getting rid of the excess water makes them light and manageable, quick to mingle with other flavours. They are particularly partial to garlic, tomatoes, and basil.

A sauce made from the latter would be delicious with aubergine fritters, which is perhaps the most common method of cooking the vegetable. Use your favourite fritter batter and ensure that it is light enough just to adhere to the sliced aubergine which must have the water extracted, otherwise the fritters will be great lumps of compressed and oily blotting paper. Fry them over a high heat, then when they are just crisp and brown drain them and serve at once.

Melitzana
2 medium-sliced aubergines
Juice from 1 lemon
2 crushed cloves of garlic
3 tablespoons olive oil
Seasoning

Bake the aubergines in a medium oven for about an hour. If they are large, the flesh comes apart from the

125

centre seeds which can then easily be discarded. Scoop out the flesh and throw away the skins. Place the flesh into a blender, add the lemon juice, garlic, seasoning, and then the oil. Blend into a smooth cream. You can make this without a blender, using a bowl and a fork, but however hard you beat the aubergine flesh it will never become as smooth or as creamy as in the blender. Sad reflection, this, on three thousand years of melitzana.

Sesame aubergines
2 medium sized aubergines
100 g/4 oz sesame seeds
100 g/4 oz sour cream
Seasoning

Roast the sesame seeds in the oven until they have become golden and released their oil (about 15 minutes depending on heat of the oven). A quicker method is to place the sesame seeds in a saucepan and to shake it over the heat — with the lid on, of course. The seeds will pop and rattle in the pan and be done in a few minutes. Add half of these to the aubergine flesh as in the above recipe, then season and stir in the sour cream. Blend for a moment or two, turn out into a dish and decorate with the rest of the sesame seeds.

Aubergine mushroom and olive purée
Flesh from 2 baked aubergines
100 g/¼ lb mushrooms
50 g/2 oz black olives
2 crushed cloves of garlic
2 tablespoons olive oil

Sauté the mushrooms in a little butter until they are soft, stone the olives and place mushrooms with their liquid, the olives, garlic seasoning and cooked pulp from the aubergines in the blender. Add the oil and reduce it to a thick cream. A very delicious purée, though you must take care that the olive flavour does not predominate.

Stuffed aubergines
2 medium sized aubergines
225 g/½ lb shallots
450 g/1 lb tomatoes
2 crushed cloves garlic
100 g/¼ lb of grated parmesan and double Gloucester mixed
Handful of breadcrumbs
Olive oil

Slice the aubergines down the centre lengthways and scoop out the flesh, leaving about ¼ cm/⅛ inch adhering to the skin. Sprinkle the inside of the skin and the cubed flesh with salt and leave to drain. Rinse well, otherwise the dish will be oversalted. Slice the shallots, peel and slice the tomatoes, crush the garlic and fry everything with the cubed aubergine flesh in a little olive oil for about 5 to 8 minutes, or until the vegetables are soft. Pile the mixture into the aubergine shells, sprinkle with the cheese and then the bread-crumbs and bake in a pre-heated medium oven for 30 minutes; or until the inside is bubbling and the top browned.

BEDSIT TREATS

Cooking for oneself in a bedsit does have its advantages. One can fail without losing face and one can experiment with odd combinations, sometimes achieving a dish that no one else has thought of. A girl I knew swore that her sardine pâté made with a teaspoon of crushed coriander and a slug of gin was better than anything served at Wheelers.

The first mistake everyone makes is thinking the most delicious meal can be created by a combination of three tins and a packet of frozen peas. In fact, you don't need to rely on tins and convenience foods at all. With a range of fresh vegetables, eggs and cheeses, you can prepare and cook a variety of good things, even on a single gas ring. But having a few herbs and spices at hand is a blessing. An indulgent relative might help to provide that first store cupboard.

A good quality mustard is a necessity. Delicatessens now stock a wide range of different mustards. Some are made with malt vinegar but I dislike them. Culpepers have the most delicious mustards of all.

My other indispensables would be a pepper mill and a supply of pepper corns, a packet of sea salt, a garlic crusher, a jar of Hungarian paprika, a packet of celery salt, sesame seeds, and a bottle of shoyu (natural soy) sauce. I would also stock up on a can or bottle of virgin olive oil and a bottle of French wine vinegar.

With these and the best fresh vegetables, one could live off a variety of salads. But that might become a little depressing. The occasional luxury can be provided with a tin of asparagus spears or artichoke hearts and 100 g/¼ lb pistachio nuts. They can all be used in omelettes and the hearts can also be dipped in batter and fried. If you want to make pasta, buy the whole or buckwheat types (they have real flavour and are nutritious) and also buy some fresh herbs, so that the cooked pasta can be tossed in oil and finely chopped parsley, basil or mint.

The recipes here are all simple to make. There are various cream cheeses mixed with herbs and spices sold in shops at absurd prices. It is well worth making your own from curd cheese and finding the flavours you prefer.

The fried cheese sandwich is popular in Southern Italy. It is one of the most delicious of all snacks, but take care and choose the best bread and fillings.

Cheese spread
285 g/10 oz curd cheese
4 finely chopped spring onions
2 chopped gherkins
1 tablespoon capers

1 tablespoon paprika
50 g/2 oz softened butter
Pinch of sea salt

Mix all ingredients together. The spread will keep covered in a refrigerator, but if it is to spread nicely it should be left at room temperature for about 15 minutes. A more nutritious cheese can be easily made by adding a well drained packet of Morinaga tofu, now available at Wholefood shops.

Fried sandwich *(makes 2)*
4 slices of crustless wholemeal bread
1 beaten egg
A good portion of the cheese spread (see above)
Butter for frying

Have a good 1 cm/¼ inch of the cheese mixture spread on the bread and press the slices gently together to make two sandwiches. Lay them in the beaten egg and leave for 30 minutes, then turn them and allow the upper side of the sandwich to soak up the egg. Fry the sandwiches in the butter until they are crisp and golden brown. The inside should just melt a little.

These sandwiches are splendid, too, if spread with bel paese, but a hard English cheese will not cook through and melt sufficiently.

Omelette with pistachio nuts
3 eggs
50 g/2 oz pistachio nuts
25 g/1 oz butter
1 tablespoon single cream
Salt and pepper

Cook the shelled nuts in the butter for a moment, pour on the lightly beaten eggs and seasoning, then add the cream. Cook for a few moments over a moderate heat. When the eggs are just cooked through, fold the omelette over and slip it out of the pan.

Tabbouleh is the classic salad of the Middle East and though the ingredients below are the correct ones, it would do the salad no harm if you added finely chopped watercress, chives, or any other fresh herb you happen to have. Do not be put off trying this recipe because the main ingredient sounds obscure. Bulgar wheat can be purchased at all well-stocked wholefood shops. If your local has not got around to stocking the grain, ask them to do so. It is a marvellously refreshing salad, very easy to make and economical; be generous with the lemon juice, onions and parsley and mint.

Tabbouleh

130 g/5 oz bulgar wheat
1 bunch of spring onions
1 generous bunch each of parsley and mint
Juice from 1 lemon
2 or 3 coarsely chopped tomatoes
80 ml/3 fl oz olive oil
Sea salt and freshly ground pepper

Pour the wheat into a bowl and cover by a good inch with cold water. Leave for two hours or more until it has soaked up all the water. Place in a sieve and squeeze it down to get rid of excess water. Chop the parsley, mint and onions as fine as you can, put the bulgar wheat into a large bowl, stir in the herbs, oil and lemon juice. Taste and season.

To serve, have the heart of a good lettuce and arrange the leaves in a circle on a large platter. Pile the tabbouleh in the centre.

ROULADES

A roulade is a roll. Almost anything — meat, fish, eggs and vegetables — that can be stuffed and then rolled, becomes a roulade. A beef olive is essential a *roulade de boeuf*. A swiss roll is also a roulade and there are various party foods, like smoked salmon rolled with brown bread and butter that are called roulades. The dish lends itself to cold buffets and summer luncheons because roulades look so attractive.

You will need a swiss roll tin, or you can improvise and make out of greaseproof paper a shallow baking tin shape which can then be used on a baking sheet. The size you need is about 30 × 22.5 cm/12 × 9 inches and both the tin or baking sheet and the paper must be well greased before cooking.

The two roulades here may seem a bit of a song and dance. A *roulade de porc*, where the loin is boned, then stuffed, rolled and roasted, is child's play compared with the gymnastic ploys with the greaseproof paper necessary here. But once you have mastered the knack of turning the roulade upside down (so that the cooked top in the oven becomes the outside of the roll) and avoided the temptation of over-filling it (so that it cannot roll neatly) and made sure that the roulade is pliable enough to roll without being so soft that it breaks — then you will have accomplished another small art of the kitchen.

It will not hurt the first roulade to be made completely out of spinach if you have no sorrel. You will find the green peppercorns give the second roulade a hot smoky taste, which may not endear itself to some palates. If so, leave them out and double the amount of olives.

Roulade d'épinards

For the roulade:

400 g/14 oz spinach leaves
200 g/7 oz sorrel leaves
4 eggs separated
100 g/4 oz double Gloucester or sage Derby cheese grated
1 tablespoon plain flour
2 tablespoons grated parmesan
Seasoning

For the filling:

225 g/8 oz ricotta cheese
A generous handful each of finely chopped parsley and mint
40 g/1½ oz butter
1 tablespoon flour
140 ml/¼ pint milk infused with bay leaves, shallot and 5 peppercorns

Tear the spinach and sorrel leaves away from their stalks. Discard the stalks. Wash the leaves, drain them and shake off all the excess water. Then cram them into a saucepan, place a tight-fitting lid on and cook over a small flame for five minutes, stirring once or twice. When soft and reduced to a purée, drain them in a sieve, gently squeezing out the liquid. Return to a dry pan and add the flour, stirring over a modest heat. Let the flour cook and thicken the purée a little.

Divide the yolks from the whites and when the purée is cool, stir in the yolks and the grated double Gloucester (or sage Derby) cheese, beating and mixing the mixture well. Season. Whip the whites of eggs until stiff and fold them into the purée.

Grease the swiss roll tin and butter or oil the greaseproof paper laid over the tin. Make sure that it is really well oiled, because bits of charred paper sticking to the dish can be a disaster. Pre-heat the oven to 425°F/218°C/Gas Mark 7. Spread the purée over the prepared tin and place in the oven for 15 to 20 minutes, or until it is crisp at the edges and bouncy in the centre. Stick a knife in the middle and if it comes out clean the roulade is cooked through.

To make the filling: infuse the milk with a couple of bay leaves, some sliced shallots or crushed garlic and the peppercorns by adding them to the milk, heating it and then allowing it to stand in a warm place for an hour. Remove the herbs before adding the milk to the butter and flour which have been melted and mixed to a roux. Beat till smooth.

Chop the parsley and mint finely and add it to the ricotta cheese. Mix well, add to the sauce and stir, allowing it to heat but not to boil. Keep warm while you take out the cooked roulade. Have a fresh piece of greaseproof paper ready sprinkled with the grated parmesan. Lift the paper at one end with the roulade upon it, so it flops over on the the parmesan paper and then peel off the paper it has cooked on. Smooth the filling over the roulade, but not right to the edges. Nick the edges at each side about 1 cm/½inch from the bottom. Then, lifting the paper beneath, roll the roulade. Once the first section is tucked under it will roll easily. Serve at once.

Roulade de poivre vert
For the roulade:
4 eggs separated
25 g/1 oz tin green peppercorns
200 g/7 oz strong flavoured, hard cheese (Wensleydale, Lancashire, double Gloucester)
3 tablespoons yoghurt
12 black olives, stoned and chopped
2 tablespoons grated parmesan
For the filling:
325 g/11 oz leeks
200 g/7 oz ricotta or low fat cheese
1 tablespoon olive oil
Generous bunch of parsley
Seasoning

133

Drain the peppercorns from their brine and add them to the grated cheese, egg yolks, yoghurt and chopped olives. Mix well. Whip the whites until stiff and fold them into the mixture. Pre-heat the oven to 425°F/ 218°C/Gas Mark 7 and continue as for the *roulade d'epinards*.

Meanwhile, chop the leeks very finely and cook them in the olive oil in a closed pan for about 5 minutes, or until they are soft. Chop the parsley and mix it into the ricotta, add this to the softened leeks. Season and keep warm.

Take the roulade out of the oven and follow the instructions above.

Both roulades are superb cold with salad, if there is any left over.

PASTA SAUCE

I believe all forms of pasta taste more delicate and are more refreshingly palatable for not being cooked with a meat-based sauce. I thought this some years ago even before I discovered that vegetarianism was a more delicious way of sustaining life. With something as modest as a paste made from flour, egg and water, meat tends to swamp it and especially if the pasta is home made. Meat, like curry powder, triumphs over all other flavours. So does the commercially made and ubiquitous tomato purée; too many recipes contain it as an ingredient and I suspect use it as a short cut to flavour. When this happens all the sauces taste much the same.

Neither should one use grated parmesan out of the packet — it has as much flavour as freeze-blown sawdust. Much better to grate up a chunk of good strong cheddar or any other of our mature cheeses. I am an English cheese chauvinist and urge the habit of using many more of them for cooking. A pasta purist would use equal quantities of fresh parmesan and gruyère mixed together.

A pasta purist would also take the spaghetti in the most

simple way, that is, tossed in good olive oil and eaten with half a dozen cloves of chopped raw garlic. Maybe you have to be addicted to garlic, as I am to enjoy that dish. But I am also addicted to the herb sweet basil, and Italian pasta dishes are redolent with this most sublime mixture, the fiery aroma or garlic and the pastoral spicy scent of basil. It is not difficult to grow in England (though people say it is), but you must choose the sunniest position indoors. Sow a packet of seeds in April. They will germinate in a couple of weeks. You will then be able to pluck the basil leaves all through the summer and autumn, and more particularly have the main ingredients for pesto, one of the great sauces of the world.

However, a sauce made out of fresh tomatoes and precious little else is a near second for culinary sensation. This is contrary to nearly all recipes for *salsa di pomodoro* which use a variety of ingredients: sugar, garlic, onions, thyme, cloves, nutmeg, parsley, red wine, carrots, celery and lord knows what else. You will achieve a perfectly good sauce with that lot, but it will not be the same as the untarnished intense flavour of the tomato sauce below.

These sauces can be used with spaghetti, macaroni, rigatoni, fettucine, tagliatelle (there must be nearly a hundred different varieties of pasta) but I bet they don't make vermicelli as they did in the 19th century: with eggs, saffron, and cheese. Sounds bliss and I would have eaten it just with a little oil and raw garlic.

Tomato sauce
450 g/1 lb tomatoes
3 cloves crushed garlic
50 g/2 oz butter
1 tablespoon olive oil
Seasoning
Wine glass of dry sherry

Do not peel the tomatoes, it is the skins that give the sauce so much flavour. Melt the butter in the oil in a thick-bottomed saucepan, add garlic, tomatoes, seasoning and sherry, stick the lid on and stop worrying for eight minutes, when it can be taken from its low flame and left to cool. Blend, then strain, throw out pips and bits of skin. You should have about 550 ml/ 1 pint of sauce. Place it again over a low flame and reduce by a third to concentrate the flavour. Enough for six generous helpings.

Mushroom sauce

225 g/¹/₂lb mushrooms
25 g/1 oz butter
1 tablespoonful olive oil
Seasoning
1 small chopped onion

Never peel mushrooms. Rinse them clean under a cold tap and put all the ingredients in a saucepan over a low flame. It is cooked in five minutes. Cool, blend, then strain. You will have a rich, creamy sauce.

Pesto

Handful of basil leaves
100 g/4 oz pine nuts
3 cloves crushed garlic
25 g/1 oz parmesan
140 ml/¹/₄ pint olive oil

With an electric blender this sauce is simplicity itself. Blend basil leaves, nuts and garlic, so that they are shredded bits, then add the olive oil gradually while blending. Pour into a bowl, add the cheese and taste for seasoning. It should have the consistency of double cream and its colour is verdant. With no electric blender, it is a matter of crushing leaves, nuts and garlic into a paste with a pestle and mortar; best done slowly while Om chanting in lotus position.

GALETTES

There have been two occasions recently when I have eaten out at restaurants specializing in nouvelle cuisine, and though impressed by the delicate purity of the food and its presentation, my palate has been lulled to a gentle comatose state where nothing, no herb or spice or — perish the thought — sliver of raw garlic could possibly enflame it into a gourmet celebration. I might add that being a guest (for like at least 50 million other people in the United Kingdom I cannot afford to eat even a baked turnip outside the home) I could hardly enquire from the chef why everything seemed to be either tinted semolina or recycled baby foods — though garnished with flair.

I know I should be relieved and grateful that at long last the trendy movement in cooking treats vegetables with the respect they have long deserved; where each vegetable is considered on its own merits, in prime condition, and is never over-cooked. That is something the English have long been waiting for. When the vegetables are accompanying meat or fish then their simplicity is possibly right and not monotonous. But even when nouvelle cuisine takes vegetables and makes a terrine or a mousse, then the end result too often is over-bland and I wonder why the diners are not in high chairs and wearing bibs.

It could be argued that my palate has lost all appreciation of the finer subtleties in flavours, but I feel that if we are to enjoy vegetables as main courses then they need to be helped with more herbs and spices, with eggs and unusual cooking cheeses, with rich sauces, different pastries and doughs and all the varied methods of cooking techniques from the wok to the barbecue.

The galette below derives from my own frustration at nouvelle cuisine. No one could complain that it is bland — the herbs, summer savory and basil are strong and distinct in themselves yet they in no way swamp the vegetables. I have had to use a French term for there is no English name for a dish that is not a pie or a gratin.

A variety of cucumber called zeppelin which grows fat rather than long is a perfect shape for the stuffed cucumber recipe to go with it. Cucumbers can be cooked and stuffed with almost any mixture of flavourings. Anne Willan of La Varenne has a recipe for *concombres farcis aux duxelles,* but I had no mushrooms; so I made this stuffing from shallots, but you may well have no shallots, so use spring onions instead: cook the white part and add the green with the parsley at the end.

Galette de choufleur
100 g/¼lb sorrel or spinach leaves
50 g/2 oz curd cheese
100 g/¼ lb sage Derby cheese
6 eggs
Teaspoon summer savory
1 large cauliflower
550 ml/1 pint tomato sauce
Handful of basil
Seasoning

First make the tomato sauce by following the recipe for tomato soup on page 108 (do not reduce it – the egg yolks will thicken it); add the finely-chopped basil to it. Purée the sorrel or spinach by putting the leaves into a pan without water or butter and letting it steam over a low heat. The sorrel will disintegrate within a few moments but the spinach will need more time. You can always cook the spinach until soft and then blend it. Add the curd cheese to the sorrel/spinach purée when it is warm so that it melts. Leave to cool; add the grated sage Derby cheese. Separate the yolks from the whites of the eggs and add the unbeaten whites, a little salt and pepper and the teaspoon of summer savory — mix well.

Now break up the cauliflower into its flowerets and boil in a little salted water for two minutes: drain (the cauliflower should still be *al dente*).

Have your shallow baking dish well buttered. (An earthenware one would be best, but I made this in a Pyrex dish.) Pour in the sorrel/spinach mixture, so that it covers the whole of the base of the dish, then arrange the cauliflower over it. Mix the six egg yolks into the tomato and basil sauce and pour that over the cauliflower so that each floweret is just covered. Place foil over the whole dish and bake in the oven for 30 minutes at 400°F/200°C/Gas Mark 6, and take the foil off for the last five minutes. Serve while it is still warm as a main dish, or it can be eaten cold.

Stuffed cucumbers
1 large cucumber
225 g/½ lb shallots or spring onions
50 g/2 oz butter
Handful of parsley
2 tablespoons breadcrumbs
1 egg
275 ml/½ pint of milk
25 g/1 oz of flour
75 g/3 oz double Gloucester cheese

Peel the cucumber in strips so that it is pleasantly striped, slice it across in four inch pieces and then down the middle; extract all the seeds and throw them away. Boil the cucumber pieces in salted water for no longer than four minutes and drain them well.

Slice the shallots or spring onions and fry them in 25 g/1 oz of butter until soft. When cool, add the chopped parsley, salt and pepper, the beaten egg and enough breadcrumbs for the mixture to hold together. Place the cucumber pieces in a buttered baking dish and spoon in the mixture to fill each piece, cook in a heated oven until the stuffing has set, about 10 to 15 minutes.

They can now be left up to 24 hours until the last stage when the sauce mornay is made.

Melt 25 g/1 oz of butter, add the flour and let the roux cook over a modest flame; season and add the milk slowly, then the cheese, and go on stirring until the sauce is smooth. Spoon on enough sauce to cover each piece of stuffed cucumber. Place in a hot oven until the sauce has browned, about 15 minutes. If it has not, place it under the grill, for if left too long to heat up the cucumber will over-cook.

MUSHROOMS

A good autumn for mushrooms and fungi follows a very wet summer, a dry August then more rain, which makes perfect conditions for the spores to thrive.

We look upon all fungi which are not field mushrooms with great suspicion. There are several thousand different varieties of fungi growing on our islands and only around 20 are poisonous, but like most people I do not find that as reassuring as I should. To be sure of knowing which ones are poisonous you need a reference book with clear, coloured drawings or photographs which describes in detail the most common fungi that grow in our woods and fields.

I rely on *British and European Mushrooms and Fungi* by Andreas Neuner (Chatto and Windus). I also use the excellent *Food for Free* by Richard Mabey, (Fontana/Collins). My rules for identification are simple. If I am not absolutely certain (and fungi at different stages of growth can look quite unlike the photograph or description), then I ignore it until I am sure. I err on the cautious side and generally check in both books.

Without doubt, the most delicious is the giant puffball which grows in woods, fields and under hedges. It can be the size of a football, or even larger, and should be creamy white on the outside. If it is turning to shades of yellow and green, it is getting old. Every part can be eaten (it need not be peeled.) Slice about $\frac{1}{2}$ cm/$\frac{1}{4}$ inch thick and fry in butter on both sides for a few minutes, until just a little crisp and brown. There is no flavour quite like it, though Richard Mabey finds it reminiscent of sweetbreads.

I also have a great enthusiasm for parasol mushrooms (and the similar shaggy parasol). These have a tall stem and the cap has an oriental shape, like part of the decoration of the Brighton Pavilion. The stalk is too fibrous to be edible, but the cap lightly fried is delicious and because of its shape and size (once I picked one 25 cm/10 inches in diameter) it is perfect for stuffing and baking in the oven.

Although I recommend simple frying in butter for most of the edible fungi as the best culinary introduction to a new food, I do think we British are over timid and unadventurous in the way we cook cultivated mushrooms. The recipes below derive from Holland, France and Austria, in that order, where people stride out into the woods with baskets and knives on weekend fungi explorations.

Mushroom soup
50 g/2 oz butter
200 g/7 oz mushrooms, cultivated or field
100 g/4 oz shallots or spring onions
25 g/1 oz butter or 2 tablespoons olive oil
1100 ml/2 pints stock or water
Juice from 1 lemon
Glass of dry sherry
2 tablespoons double cream, or 2 tablespoons of yoghurt

Slice mushrooms, shallots or spring onions, and melt butter in a saucepan. Add vegetables, let them cook a little, and then add the stock, sherry, and lemon juice. Cover the pan, simmer for 5 minutes, add seasoning, and stir in the cream or yoghurt before serving.

Stuffed mushrooms

8 large mushrooms, cultivated, field or parasol
100 g/4 oz brown breadcrumbs
50 g/2 oz butter
3 sliced shallots or 5 spring onions
2 crushed cloves of garlic
Handful of chopped parsley
2 teaspoons chopped marjoram
2 tablespoons dry white wine
Sea salt and black pepper.

Take the stalks from the mushrooms (if parasol, discard). Chop and sauté stalks in half of the butter with the shallots or spring onions and the garlic, until they are soft. Add the breadcrumbs, parsley, marjoram, wine, and seasoning, and mix well. Butter a baking dish with the rest of the butter, spread the mixture on each mushroom and bake in a moderately hot oven 375°F/193°C/Gas Mark 5 for 30 minutes. Serves 4.

Paprika mushrooms

450 g/1 lb mushrooms, cultivated or field
50 g/2 oz butter or 2 tablespoons olive oil
4 peeled tomatoes
2 crushed cloves of garlic
2 teaspoons of mild paprika
140 ml/5 fl oz sour cream or yoghurt
Juice from 1 lemon
Sea salt and black pepper

Chop the mushrooms and peeled tomatoes coarsely and sauté, in the butter with the garlic until they are soft. Add the paprika, lemon juice, sour cream and seasoning, and cook for another moment stirring well.

Winter

If you do not live in a city or a large town or at weekly striking distance of a market which sells imported vegetables, then your range of food at first sight appears to be limited. City dwellers are spoilt in the sense of having fresh salad all the year round. There are now splendid iceberg and Webb's wonder lettuces imported from California and Israel which, considering hardly any of the leaves need to be thrown away, are excellent value. In London markets you can buy throughout the winter tomatoes, aubergines, peppers, courgettes; in fact, if you were willing to pay the price you could cook ratatouille or pipérade as easily in January as in June.

But our bodily needs change with the seasons: if it is 5 degrees below zero, we are not going to be delighted at the propect of a green salad for lunch. What we want from winter meals is warmth, more carbohydrate, more grains and pulses, more hot thick soups, more spicy vegetable stews, more curries with brown rice. And if we eat salads, they will be those good crisp winter ones, with finely chopped fresh cabbage, brussels sprouts, grated carrots, thinly sliced onions, mixed with grains and seeds.

In one sense — that of economy — it is almost better to stick to the vegetables which the season offers; also the macrobiotic school of thought has influenced to some degree current vegetarian thinking. This considers the body to be happiest if it keeps to the foods grown in its local climatic habitat. This notion taken logically would mean that we in the British Isles (belonging to northwest Europe) could never eat citrus fruits or a host of other foods. I have no views on this either way; there has been no scientific research done upon the hypothesis, but I do find myself sympathetic to the macrobiotic point of view. Certainly it does the body no harm at all to restrict the diet to a limited range of food.

For this reason our own root vegetables — turnips, parsnips, swedes, beetroots and carrots — come into their own in the winter months. There is too, in our country, the largely-ignored celeriac. (Sainsbury's now stock it from the beginning of autumn.) This is a white bulbous root which tastes of the nutty base of celery. In France, it is common; they grate it and mix it with mayonnaise. The root should be small as should all root vegetables for the best flavour. We tend to allow all of our vegetables to grow into monsters — as if they are all going to be prize winners at the harvest festival — but over a moderate size they quickly become tough and lose flavour. Buy all root vegetables small and firm. Turnips, again much prized in France, are delicious if fresh and small.

Root vegetables are largely associated in our mind with meat stews, where their porous consistency soaks up the fats and meat flavours. They will, of course, do that with olive oil, cooked with herbs and spices, and still remain distinct in taste. Beetroots have to be considered separately, as they turn everything else purple.

The great standby in winter is the huge and varied pulse family. Wholefood shops now stock many more kinds than they did a few years ago. It is worth sampling them, then buying your favourite ones in bulk to save money. If you are in a hurry the very small beans, peas and lentils need no soaking at all. But even these will take kindly to a ten minute soaking when they will double or triple their bulk. You can leave the bigger beans to soak overnight if you wish, though I often pour boiling water over them, leave

144

them for an hour, and then start to cook them. Pour the soaking water away.

Do not use long slow cooking for any beans, especially red kidney beans. Because of several outbreaks of food poisoning it is now known that red kidney beans contain a toxin (Phaseolus vulgaris) which is increased by cooking at a low temperature for a length of time. But it is destroyed by boiling for ten minutes. Other legumes contain the toxin in very much smaller quantities.

This should not be alarming — even though the Bulgarian broadcaster Georgy Markov was killed by a similar poison (administered via an injection from an umbrella) which derived from the castor oil bean — for all foods contain toxins in various quantities. The amounts are so small that our bodies quickly neutralize the toxins. I have eaten red kidney beans for many years and never suffered a moment's disquiet.

Thick vegetable and bean soup
Root vegetables and pulses together make the best soups in the world. It almost makes winter worthwhile to sit down to a bowl of thick vegetable and bean soup with warm home-made wholemeal bread.

Here are a few suggestions for soups:
Carrot, onion and haricot bean, flavoured with carraway or dill.
Parsnip, leek and lima bean, flavoured with fennel seed.
Turnip, cabbage, garlic and black-eyed bean soup.
Cauliflower, flageolet and parsley soup.
Onion and green lentil soup.
Onion, butter bean and mung bean soup.

Use about 600 g/1 lb 6 oz vegetables to 285 g/10 oz dried beans. Soak the beans. It is best to cook the beans and the vegetables separately, then combine in whatever quantities you wish. If not, the saucepan becomes too full and beans, lentils or potatoes may well stick and burn. Also, once the beans or lentils are cooked you can gauge the consistency of the soup better.

Do not peel the vegetables, as much of the vitamins and minerals will be lost. Cook them in boiling water, without salt, for whatever length of time is needed, having diced them reasonably small.

Cook the pulses in another saucepan, by adding them to a tablespoon of olive oil in which the spices have been sautéed. Add at least 1100 ml/2 pints of water, also unsalted, and let them simmer for an hour or more.

Combine the two in whatever ratio you want and flavour by adding either salt and black pepper, or shoyu, tamari or a little miso paste.

COOKING VEGETABLES

We tend to dismiss vegetables as not being quite the raw material for haute cuisine — the French and the Chinese being the exceptions — nor has it helped that vegetarians gave to their meals a nutty glow of wholesomeness which sounded a bit bland and stodgy. But vegetables have a wide and varied range of flavour and texture, they can be cooked, hot and crisp within a few moments, stir-fried, steamed, poached, sautéed, boiled. They also adapt beautifully to slow cooking where they can soak up the herbs, spices and oils.

Whatever method of cooking is used the flavour of the particular vegetable will vary, because the chemical structure is being broken down at a different rate with a different heat: this alters the flavour. Every cook continually tastes and checks the food — overcooking can be a second too long. The flavour can obviously further be changed by the oil or butter in which the vegetable is cooking and any herbs or spices added to the butter or oil beforehand.

Vegetables are very obliging, most are delicious raw and

under-cooked, yet at the other extreme they purée easily and their flavour is altered again. In that state they will fuse with gleeful abandon with eggs, cream and all manner of cheeses. Some vegetables, I've noticed, have an affinity with particular cheeses: spinach for example insists upon sage Derby, while onions are fond of double Gloucester.

I have to admit that the boiling and over-cooking of vegetables distresses me; I feel it to be mass slaughter of the unprotected. Spinach and leeks are both misused in this manner and end up as soggy, mangled lumps, their flavour and nutriment having been thrown down the sink.

After washing a pound of spinach squeeze out the water still clinging to the leaves with your hands. Melt 25 g/1 oz of butter in a heavy saucepan, add the spinach and seasoning, place a close-fitting lid on the saucepan and cook over a low heat. After two minutes stir the spinach with a wooden spoon and shove the top, uncooked part down to the bottom. After four to five minutes the spinach should have contracted to one-third of its bulk and is ready to be served. But if you wish it to be completely tender or to purée the spinach, let it remain over the flame for another minute, or until the spinach is a quarter of its original bulk. Then it will have to be drained and you can use its liquor for a sauce or reserve it for soup stock.

Much of the secret of cooking leeks is in the preparation. There is a lot of nonsense talked about only eating the white part. You discard the green fibrous leaves certainly, but much of the pale green top of the leek is as good as the white base. Cut the leek lengthways down the middle so that you expose all the interior to the cold water tap and remove all the mud. Then slice the leeks across in one-inch segments, heat a tablespoon of olive oil in a saucepan, add the leeks and seasoning, place over a low heat and within four to five minutes they will have halved their bulk and be ready for the table. Don't let them go mushy. Even for making soup one would start off cooking the vegetables in this manner, for it intensifies the flavour and ensures that no goodness is lost.

Chicory can be cooked in a similar fashion, but do not cut it with a steel knife because that increases the bitterness of the leaves. A perfect and trouble-free way is to bake it, then you don't have to prepare the vegetable at all. Wipe the chicory with a damp cloth, and lay them in a heavily buttered oven dish with a lid, place that into a moderate oven and cook for 45 minutes. Scoop out the centre of the vegetable at the table, leaving the base and tougher outer leaves. It will have a creamy consistency and a heavenly flavour.

BEANS

In the winter months I use more dried beans. Here is another common myth: we are constantly told to soak dried beans and peas overnight. Yet if you pour boiling water upon them they will triple their bulk within 15 minutes. If they don't, it means they are old stock and will be tough even when they have been stewing for hours.

The large white haricot beans, fagioli, are one of the most delicious of pulses. Meat eaters flavour the beans with garlic and rosemary and cook them with lamb; the Greeks make fasoulia out of them; the Italians a Tuscan bean and pasta soup and also eat them cold with tuna fish as a salad. Here is a soup recipe where half is puréed to make a thick creamy sauce, which I've enriched and intensified here by adding garlic hollandaise. Allow your guests the sybaritic pleasure of spooning the hollandaise into their soup bowls at the table and have a dish of winter savory or chopped parsley to go with it.

Zuppa di fagioli
350 g/12 oz white haricot beans
225 g/8 oz onions
1 whole celery
50 g/2 oz butter
2 tablespoons olive oil
Seasoning

Cook the soaked beans in 1650 ml/3 pints of water. They should be tender within two hours, but check, for they may need a little more water as they are cooking. Meanwhile, chop the onions and celery and cook those separately in the butter and oil, with the seasoning, in a closed pan over a low heat. They will be tender within 20 minutes. Mix the beans with the vegetables and blend half of the soup into a smooth cream. Then add the puréed soup to the rest of the soup. Serve with dollops of the hollandaise garlic sauce in the individual soup bowls.

Hollandaise garlic sauce
3 egg yolks
Juice from 1 lemon
3 cloves of garlic, crushed
Seasoning
170 g/6 oz melted butter

To save the tedium of making this sauce in a double boiler try using a blender. Mix yolks, lemon, garlic and seasoning together, then slowly add the melted butter, blending quickly at the same time. Continue for a few minutes until the sauce thickens.

If you are not eating meat you can afford to buy a thick well-flavoured olive oil. Fasoulia is a dish that needs it.

Fasoulia
350 g/12 oz dried haricot beans
140 ml/¼ pint olive oil
5 cloves of garlic, peeled
1 bay leaf
Pinch of thyme, and sage
1 teaspoon oregano
2 tablespoons tomato purée
1 onion chopped
Juice from 1 lemon

Soak, then drain the beans. Heat the olive oil in a thick-bottomed saucepan. Throw in the beans with the garlic, bay leaf, thyme, sage and oregano. Let the beans simmer for up to 10 minutes so that they begin to soak up the oil and herbs, then add enough boiling water to cover them by 3 cm/an inch or so. Stir in the tomato purée and let them cook very slowly for about 2 hours. When they are tender, add the raw chopped onion and the lemon juice, stir that into the beans, put the lid back on the saucepan, take it away from the heat and leave for another 10 minutes before serving.

The black bean stew is hot and spicy, hearty fare for the winter months. I could write many an essay in praise of dried beans, peas or lentils, for their variery of shape and colour seduce the palate, but they do need a lot of help in the final stages of cooking from herbs, spices, butter, and good olive oil. Plain boiled they are boringly bland, yet for most of their cooking time they must be plain boiled and nothing else.

Salt must be added after the beans are cooked or their outer skins will harden, so if cooked in stock it must be unsalted. Herbs, spices, and olive oil can be added from the earliest stages of cooking, but in my experience it makes little difference to the final taste. I prefer to boil the beans in a lot of water, strain them after 10 minutes, then strain them again when they are finally cooked through. After that, all the extra flavours can be added and another half hour's cooking will not harm them.

Straining the beans after they have boiled for 10 minutes is a newish theory, to do with the matter of their indigestibility, as people delicately put it. And it is certainly a pity to have to avoid beans because of colonic maelstrom. Try washing them before soaking, straining the soaking water from them, then straining again after 10 minutes fierce boiling. I cannot promise a fart-free post-bean day, but it ought to help. (There is, however, a more important reason for boiling the beans and throwing the water away.

It has recently been discovered that beans contain a toxin which is destroyed in this initial boiling. The toxin was discovered in red kidney beans, when some misguided people ate soaked raw beans in a salad and became ill.)

I am also rather against soaking the beans overnight. I prefer to pour boiling water over the dried beans, and usually within 15 minutes they will triple their bulk. It is impossible to give exact cooking times for dried beans or peas. It very much depends upon their age and how long they have been kept upon the shop shelves. Try to buy all the dried pulses from stores which have a continual turnover of goods. They should be bright and shining — if they look dull they have been around for too long.

English celery is at its best in winter and the outside fibrous leaves, deliciously nutty in flavour, make a fine vegetable stock.

Black bean stew
350 g/12 oz dried black beans
1100 ml/2 pints celery stock
2 large onions
1 large parsnip
50 g/2 oz grated ginger root
1 teaspoon chilli powder
1 teaspoon each freshly ground rosemary, oregano and thyme
2 tablespoons olive oil
Sea salt and black pepper

Soak the beans. Strain them. Boil them in water for about 10 minutes, then strain them again. Stir the beans into half of the olive oil, then add the celery stock. Let them simmer on top of the stove for an hour. The beans should be still whole but soft enough to bite into.

Meanwhile have the crushed garlic, grated ginger, chilli powder, the herbs and seasoning sweat in the rest of the olive oil, so as to release all their flavours. Chop the onion and slice the parsnip fairly small, add the vegetables and the beans to the herbs and give the pan a good stir. It may well need more stock or water now. Let it simmer on top of the stove for another half hour. Taste and check for seasoning. If it still needs a little livening up, a teaspoon of tamari soy sauce or a couple of shakes from the tabasco bottle might not come amiss; though with the chilli and the ginger it ought to be hot enough for most tastes.

WINTER WARMER

I think the only thing I have missed about not eating meat is suet pud, especially in the winter, when I have thought nostalgically about suet crust on top of steak and kidney pudding, or dumplings swimming around in stew, playing dodgem cars with the carrots.

But recently I have experimented with a vegetable fat, Mapletons' Nutter, which I have grated into the flour, and I am here to tell you that not only does it make dumplings which look like tufts of whipped cream but also steamed pud that could have been mistaken from afar for a whiff of cumulus cloud, so light, feathery, and handsome did it turn out. (It does not say on the packet what vegetable oils Nutter contains, but as it is a hard fat like lard it is almost certain to contain coconut oils, high in the saturated fats. Thus it is in no way a healthier food than an animal fat. It does, however, make a far lighter suet than lard or pork dripping.)

Steamed onion pudding
225 g/8 oz self-raising flour
100 g/4 oz vegetable fat
2 large onions
Sea salt and black pepper

Sift the flour into a mixing bowl. Grate the fat into it and stir. Chop the onions and add them to the mixture with the salt and pepper. Stir again. Add enough water to make a dough — it will need only about two tablespoons, so take care.

Mix it into a ball, then either put it into a pudding basin and cook it as you would the Christmas pudding or as I did, place the whole unsavoury-looking concoction in a roasting bag, seal it and cook in a steamer. I cooked mine for all of four hours, mainly because I had no faith in its worth. But it should be cooked thoroughly within two hours, and I promise you the result is truly blissful.

But it is essential to consume the pudding with a sauce and anything with a milk base, béchamel or mornay, would strike an undesirably heavy note. A simple butter sauce would be excellent made with water and thickened with the merest teaspoon of cornflour and perhaps some chopped spring onion or parsley. I went to town with the following:

Ginger sauce
50 g/2 oz butter
50 g/2 oz grated ginger
2 crushed cloves of garlic
1 tablespoon tamari soy sauce
550 ml/1 pint water
1 teaspoon cornflour

Melt the butter and cook the grated ginger root and garlic over a gentle flame for about four minutes. Add the tamari soy sauce and the water, let it come to the boil, then add the cornflour which has been mixed with a little cold water beforehand. Taste and check it does not need a little salt.

MASH OF THE DAY

Because of the aesthetic mystique that beautiful is slim, potatoes in our time have been much maligned. They are not just fattening carbohydrate, they also contain valuable protein, fibre, minerals and vitamins. They also happen to be one of the most appetizing of all vegetables and adapt themselves stunningly to a whole range of tempting dishes — from the Greek *skordalia*, a potato and garlic mayonnaise that can scorch the roof of the mouth, to the great French classic, *gratin dauphinois*, which when cooked in wholesome simplicity just with single cream and the merest pinch of nutmeg (no garlic, cheese, milk or eggs) is one of the most sublime dishes of the world.

Crudely, potatoes may be divided up into those which are floury — they have slightly more carbohydrate in them than the others (King Edward are the most common) and the firm waxy kind which will not disintegrate when boiled — Graigs Royal and Maris Peer are two of many. However, we get little opportunity to choose in the shops. Farmers produce the potatoes that have the greatest yield and often shop assistants are ignorant of the name of the potato they are selling.

Gratin dishes need a firm potato and a shallow fireproof dish for them to cook in. A mandoline helps to slice them, but with a sharp steel knife and patience it is not a chore.

The other dishes below need a floury type of potato that will mash well, but do not let them get over-cooked or waterlogged. Watch the cooking time, drain them at once and put the saucepan back over the heat to drive out the moisture.

I was reminded of the delight of various kinds of potato croquettes, scones, fritters and cakes by noticing that Birds Eye have something on the market now called Cheesies. The manufacturers describe them as 'potato and cheddar cheese mixed in a creamy sauce wrapped in golden breadcrumbs'. I found them incredibly bland with an off-putting pappy consistency and I thought wistfully of all the delicious croquettes that could so easily be made and cost very little.

If you use nuts in cooking, the economic way is to buy in bulk and grind what you need in the blender, or crush them with a pestle and mortar, just before use.

154

Skordalia

450 g / 1 lb potatoes
5 crushed garlic cloves
Juice from 1 lemon
140 ml / ¼ pint olive oil
Salt and pepper

Peel and boil the potatoes, drain and then place back over a moderate heat, shake the pan and stir so that they dry out completely. Mash to a smooth consistency, then push them through a sieve. Stir the crushed garlic cloves into the potato, then as if making mayonnaise, add the olive oil, beating it into the potato with a fork or an egg whisk; it will soon become a smooth thick cream. Add the lemon juice after all the oil has been absorbed. Finally add the seasoning to taste. Serve lukewarm. In Greece it is traditionally eaten at Lent with slices of fried aubergine and courgette.

Gratin dauphinois

900 g / 2 lb potatoes
25 g / 1 oz butter
875 ml / 1½ pints single cream
1 teaspoon nutmeg
Salt and pepper

Peel the potatoes, cut them into slices the size and thickness of an old penny: soak the slices in cold water for 30 minutes so that they lose some of their starch. Drain and pat them dry.

Use the butter to smear the inside of a shallow earthenware dish, place a layer of potatoes inside, season, sprinkle a little of the nutmeg on, then continue with up to four or five layers, but no more. Pour the cream over the dish and leave for a few minutes, so that the cream sinks down through the layers.

Place the dish into a pre-heated oven 300°F/150°C/ Gas Mark 2 and let it cook slowly for 2½ hours.

155

I know it sounds like a hell of a lot of cream and is mad extravagance, but it is worth it. (For those of us watching our saturated fat intake, the amount of cream is scandalous, and for those of us watching our health it is not worth it. Non-fat yoghurt can be used instead of single cream, with a polyunsaturate margarine used to grease the dish. However do not fool yourself that it is then gratin dauphinois; it is something else, delicious in its own right, and similar to Indian and Middle Eastern methods of cooking potatoes.)

Potato and nut croquettes
450 g/1 lb potatoes, boiled
100 g/4 oz ground mixed nuts
1 tablespoon each mustard seed, poppy seed, sesame seed
25 g/1 oz flaked almonds
Salt and pepper

Mash the cooked potatoes. Stir over a moderate heat to drive off moisture, then add all the other ingredients except for the flaked almonds. Press the mixture flat to the depth of one inch in a shallow dish or baking tray and leave in the refrigerator for a day.

The mixture is now easy to mould. Cut into long segments, slice those into 5 cm/2 inch cork shapes, roll onto a floured board and then into the flaked almonds. Shallow fry in a little butter and oil. This amount will serve six handsomely.

There is an assumption among meat-eaters that those of us who have rejected meat for one reason or another must live on a spartan diet of beans, nuts, and grains. Fictions sometimes have a shred of truth in them and I must admit that the image of a meatless diet is often not helped by those practitioners who seem knee-deep in stodge. But if you have a sybaritic nature, a diet or a dish cannot commend itself merely because it is healthy.

So I am often asked, What do you eat? What is a typical meal?

I cannot envisage any meal being typical — so I have chosen almost at random a meal I have cooked and enjoyed. Some people are genuinely puzzled as to what one eats with what — as if once you discard the meat you must just be left with the two veg; that, I agree, would be dismal. The meat-and-two-veg. syndrome tends to put gastronomy into a straitjacket. It is far better to ignore it and pursue the oriental traditions, where many small dishes are served, the order being dictated by the cook and the demands of the kitchen and its appliances.

The two dishes below could well be part of a dinner party menu, but I would probably start with crudités and an aioli mayonnaise, followed by borsch, before the leeks and avocado. I ate the pie with a crisp green salad and nothing else, for it is surprisingly substantial. But for a dinner party for eight, I would braise some fresh celery hearts or cook some spinach *en branche*, served with a light sauce made from gruyère and skimmed milk. I would still serve the salad.

I have noticed that there are now more brands of naturally fermented soy sauce on the market. Apart from those called shoyu or tamari, there is a Japanese brand called Kikkoman. All of these make excellent sauces; one tablespoon of soy or more to 140 ml/$\frac{1}{4}$ pint of water, thickened with one teaspoon of cornflour can be the basic for added herbs or spices. In the sauce below I have added mustard powder which merges well with the soy. The fat I have used for the pastry dough is Mapletons' Nutter.

Leeks stuffed with avocado purée

4 large leeks (allow half a leek for each person)
1 avocado
Juice from 1 lemon
2 crushed cloves of garlic
140 ml/$\frac{1}{4}$ pint of olive oil
Seasoning

Trim green leaves from leeks, slice lengthways and

157

wash under a running tap. Place leeks in a steamer and cook them for about six minutes or until they are just soft. Scoop out a little of the centre of each leek, so that there is a boat-shaped indentation, and place the scooped-out pieces into a blender with a little of the olive oil. The avocado can be peeled from the outside and the flesh sliced away from the stone. Blend to a thick purée, and add a little sea salt and black pepper if you think it needs it. Spoon the purée into the leeks and sprinkle a tiny amount of finely chopped mint or parsley over the top.

Cauliflower pie

1 small cauliflower
6 shallots or small onions
2 tablespoons naturally fermented soy sauce
1 teaspoon cornflour
1 teaspoon mustard powder
140 ml/¼ pint water
For the pastry dough:
350 g/12 oz plain flour
250 g/9 oz vegetable fat
2 tablespoons iced water

Make the pastry a day before and refrigerate. Use half for the base. Roll out on a floured board, fit it into a pie dish, prick and fill with dried beans (so that the pastry does not puff up in the oven). Partially cook in a preheated oven 425°F/220°C/Gas Mark 7 for 6 to 10 minutes. Take the dried beans out for the last three minutes, so that the base is cooked through: otherwise it tends to be soggy.

Slice cauliflower into its individual florets, peel central stem and slice that too. Peel the shallots or onions and cut them in half. Boil the cauliflower in a little water for four minutes and in a steamer above cook the shallots or onions. The vegetables should still be *al dente*.

Mix the mustard powder with a little of the water in a pan so that it is a paste, put it over a low flame and add the rest of the water and the soy; when it is simmering, stir in the cornflour which has been first mixed with some water. The sauce should not be too thick. Check for flavour, and if necessary add more soy or mustard.

Arrange the cauliflower and shallots or onions on the cooked pastry shell in the dish and pour the sauce over the top. Roll out the other half of pastry dough and fit the lid to the pie. Brush with beaten egg or milk. Bake in a pre-heated oven 400°F/200°C/Gas Mark 6 for 30 minutes or until the top is golden brown. A splendid pie to be eaten cold if there is any left over.

Carnivores do not have a monopoly of good things nor, more specifically, of cunning ways of cooking so that essential flavours are sealed. I am thinking of cooking *en croûte*, where the raw food is wrapped in a pastry parcel, which goes into a hot oven, and all the cooking juices soak into the interior of the pastry; this can be one of life's tasty delights.

There is yet another delight too that the carnivores indulge in, which vegetarian cooking seems oddly modest or downright shy about. That is either cooking the food in wine or adding a little delicious booze to a sauce. So much can be improved with a tablespoon of dry sherry, vermouth or white wine: indeed, often the food can be resurrected from the stillborn blandness.

The recipes below celebrate the two delights in one. But I will confess immediately to one major cop-out. I use frozen puff pastry. It is, I believe, one of the few commercial products which is of high quality and saves many hours of chore in the kitchen. But it is essential to roll it out thinly, to one-sixteenth of an inch, it says on the packet (though I hardly think it is measurable). This is perfect for the *croûte*: the interior, wafer thin, is soft and soaks up the essential flavours while the outside is crisp and flaky.

The purpose of using wine in cooking, apart from marinating and tenderizing, is to flavour the food. You burn off the alcohol in the cooking and leave a hint of the grape behind. This is all very well, but I am not one to say no to a sauce which has not had the alcohol steamed away. In fact, I am positively devoted to a sauce which on a second helping would tempt the law to breathalyse you. I exaggerate — but only a little; what I would suggest as a general rule is to cook with the wine in the usual way and then just before serving add a teaspoon more. This intensifies the subliminal flavour. I know it may be expensive cooking with booze, but even a very little makes an enormous difference.

When cooking vegetables in a saucepan with just butter, and you need them to make their own liquor, it helps the process to add a pinch of salt at that stage.

Poireaux en croûte

675 g/1½ lb leeks
400 g/14 oz packet of puff pastry
25 g/1 oz butter
Sea salt and freshly ground pepper
For the white wine sauce:
50 g/2 oz butter
25 g/1 oz plain flour
Glass of dry white wine
140 ml/¼ pint leek stock

Heat the oven to 400°F/200°C/Gas Mark 6. Clean the leeks by cutting them lengthways, opening up each one, so that you can see where the dirt is. Cut all the fibrous leaves off and put them in a saucepan with half pint of water, boil for five minutes, then liquidize and sieve, or put them through the food mill. Strain and save all the liquid. This should give you 140 ml/¼ pint of leek stock.

Cut the leeks into 2.5 cm/1 inch lengths; place them

in a saucepan with the butter and a pinch of salt, let them cook for two minutes only, so that they are on the point of softening but no more. Drain any liquid there is into the leek stock. Leave to cool.

Make the wine sauce by adding stock and wine to the roux and stirring until it is smooth. Taste, add salt and pepper. Let the sauce chill in the refrigerator while you roll out the pastry.

Butter a shallow earthenware dish, have your pastry rolled out to twice the area of the dish with its centre inside the dish. Start building with the leek pieces on this centre, so that it is roughly a Nissen hut shape, spoon the chilled sauce over the top, (it should just rest there like snow on the peaks), then fold the pastry into the centre and let both sides overlap on the top, press gently down to seal it. Close both ends and cut any surplus pastry away.

Brush with milk or beaten egg, and pop into the oven for 30 minutes or until the whole parcel is golden brown and you can smell the aroma of wine sauce.

Choufleur en croûte
1 medium sized cauliflower
400 g/14 oz packet of puff pastry
50 g/2 oz butter
50 g/2 oz flour
275 ml/½ pint of milk
Handful of finely chopped parsley
Sea salt and pepper

Heat the oven to 400°F/200°C/Gas Mark 6. Slice the cauliflower into pieces with floweret and stalk about as large as the palm of your hand, throw them into a saucepan with a lot of boiling salted water and let them cook for two minutes (and two minutes only). Drain at once and let them cool. The cauliflower flowerets should just have begun to get tender. They will finish their cooking inside the pastry later, but even then

161

they should be still *al dente.*

A quick way of making the parsley sauce is to put the milk and parsley leaves into the blender and let the blades do the work for you. Make the roux and add the parsley milk. Let the sauce chill so that you can control it later.

Roll out the pastry as in the above recipe, pile on the pieces of cauliflower, fitting them into each other as best you can. It will not be a tidy shape but that won't effect the lustre of the final croûte. Spoon on the sauce and fold the pastry over. Cook as above.

Champignons en croûte
325 g/11 oz mushrooms
50 g/2 oz butter
400 g/14 oz packet of puff pastry
1 teaspoon cornflour
Seasoning

Heat the oven to 400°F/200°C/Gas Mark 6. Wash and break up the mushrooms into small pieces. Cook them in a saucepan with the butter for a few moments until they are soft and are steeped in their own liquid thicken them with the cornflour, and put aside to chill.

Roll out the pastry as in the above recipes, spoon the mushrooms in and make your sealed parcel. Bake until golden brown, about 30 minutes.

PANCAKES

Though pancakes appear to be popular, and getting more so from the evidence of the crêperies which are flourishing around London, I wonder if we often cook them at home, or eat them in any other way than the tradition of Shrove Tuesday, where we still enjoy them as a pudding with lemon and caster sugar.

Savoury pancakes are another mouth-watering pleasure altogether. A thin envelope enclosing a creamy vegetable

162

purée possibly delights the palate because each enhances the other. We can flavour the batter itself with herbs or curry spices. We can also add a vegetable purée to the batter, and timbales de crêpes is an excellent dish where you trim and shape about 10 pancakes and fit them into a soufflé dish with a purée of vegetables between each pancake, the whole topped by a cheese sauce and baked in the oven (see page 174).

The more you think about pancakes, the more their range of usefulness to the enterprising cook grows. All very well, you might say, but first make your pancake. Here I have a slight gripe. All cookery books give amounts of flour, egg, milk and water, of melted butter and oil, which give you a pancake of light lacy thinness which is inclined to tear as you breathe upon it, and therefore cannot enfold any filling whatsoever.

Possibly these cooks are much cleverer than I am and have light fingers that caress the cooked batter in an amiable and courting fashion so that the pancake helplessly does what it should. I cannot even toss a piece of filigree lace in my pan without it breaking into flying morsels and landing in the waiting mouths of the cats below.

My batter for savoury pancakes will not tear, is easy to turn in the pan, and can be tossed with the style of a Russian gymnast. It will also fold over and enclose any filling without it oozing out and away. Unlike the crêpe batter on pages 174-5 this one has three eggs instead of two.

Savoury pancake batter
100 g/4 oz plain flour
3 eggs
275 ml/½ pint skimmed milk
½ teaspoon salt
2 tablespoons olive oil

You can put all the ingredients into a blender and turn it on for a minute, adding the olive oil last. But excellent results can be achieved with just a bowl, a wooden spoon and an egg whisk or beater: sift the flour into the bowl, make a well in the centre, break the eggs into it with the salt, stir until you get a paste and then add the milk slowly until there is no dry flour left. Then whisk or beat into a smooth liquid.

I think it is essential to leave the batter for a few hours in the refrigerator. This allows the starch cells to swell and the batter will thicken slightly. Best of all if you can leave the batter for 24 hours, but it must be well beaten again the moment before you start to cook with it.

If you want to flavour the batter, add to the flour either a teaspoon each of herbs, such as oregano, thyme and marjoram, or a tablespoon of curry spices. A teaspoon of chilli powder will give you a hot spicy batter that is not a curry flavour.

You can also subtract from the milk quantity, adding the same amount of liquid purée — spinach, mushroom or tomato. You can add ground nuts or sesame seeds to the flour, but remember that anything heavy will sink to the bottom of the bowl, so the batter will need constant beating or stirring.

Pancake-making is easier if you have a proper pan made of cast iron which keeps a steady strong heat; tossing the pancake is then a simpler operation, but it also helps if you have cast-iron forearms. However, an omelette pan will do, or an ordinary frying pan. The base diameter needs to be about 15 to 18 cm/6 to 7 inches. To cover this area you will need to measure out into a ladle about three tablespoons of batter.

There is in the writings on pancakes a lot of admonition about never frying a pancake; you just smear or wipe the pan with the fat and when it smokes, ladle the batter in. To follow this advice sometimes means burnt pans and batter that sticks and a pancake which is shared among the cats. One cookery expert says ideally the cook should wipe the pan with an artist's mahl stick, which is a mop cap of rag tied to a long pole. It is one of those useful things we all have in our kitchen somewhere. Sometimes I lie awake at night, wondering where I have put my mahl stick, so that I can wipe my pans with it.

To avoid deep and shallow frying, and burnt remnants of batter, pour into the pan about a teaspoon of oil and let it run over the base. This will do two pancakes and maybe three; then you will need another teaspoon of oil.

Heat the pan and the oil. When a little smoke begins to rise, tip the ladle of batter into the pan. Angle the pan immediately so that the batter covers the base. It will cook through in half a minute; turn or toss it; the other side will cook within a few seconds.

If you intend to stuff the pancakes, then it is best to do them all in one batch, having the filling already made hot. Place a little of it on each pancake and fold each side over so that they overlap. Arrange the stuffed pancakes on an ovenware dish and pop them into a hot oven for five to ten minutes.

One of the nicest ways of eating pancakes was one I stumbled on at a dinner party. I contrived a do-it-yourself stuffed pancake. I made a batch of hot pancakes. I had also made several purées and spicy stuffings and I left it to the guests, with everything laid out before them at the table, to choose what they would eat with what and how, with forks or fingers.

Here are a few of the fillings you could make:

Avocado purée II
The flesh from two avocados blended with a clove of crushed garlic, juice from half a lemon and two tablespoons or more of sunflower oil. Olive oil can be used and I prefer it, but the purée is thicker and stronger in flavour.

Mushroom and watercress purée
Sauté 225 g/½ lb of mushrooms in 25 g/1 oz butter in a closed saucepan until cooked (a few minutes). Chop a bunch of watercress fairly small, add it to the

mushrooms and season. Blend the lot to a thick purée and add a carton of sour cream. Stir well when you reheat it.

Egg and walnut stuffing
Hard boil four eggs: place them in a saucepan of cold water, bring to the boil, place the lid on the saucepan and leave away from the heat for 10 minutes. This is the best method of ensuring that the eggs are cooked without having to chew on white rubber. Slice and mash the eggs. Add 100 g/4 oz of ground walnuts, salt and pepper.

The idea was, and it worked, that guests would spread a little of the avocado or the mushroom and watercress purée on the pancake, then sprinkle one of the stuffings over that, then roll or fold their pancake.

Lastly, try this for an appetizer. Make the batter with the herbs or the curry spices in it, measure out a tablespoon of batter so that each pancake is quite small. When they are done, spread each one with soured cream and roll them up. Good warm or cool and they certainly make a change from an unidentified thing on a biscuit.

GARLIC

People are still suspicious of garlic and tend to use it nervously, are stingy with the amount and unadventurous as to where and how they use it. They do not always realize how radically garlic is changed by being cooked and also that the larger cloves now available are far milder in taste.

Garlic has a long history of distrust and taboo as well as being held in reverential awe. Because of the arrangement of the cloves rotating around the central core it had a crude cosmic parallel; it was sometimes used as currency and often for swearing oaths. For centuries it was part of the staple diet of the great mass of working people.

Do not be put off from trying any of the following

recipes because of the chore of peeling garlic; use the same method as for skinning tomatoes. Separate the cloves, pour boiling water over them, leave them for a minute of two and then slice the bottom of each clove and the skin will fall away.

I use about two crushed cloves of garlic in a sauce vinaigrette for a green salad for four to six people. I was never much impressed with the idea of a clove of garlic smeared on the salad bowl itself. The most efficient garlic crusher I have discovered is made in France and has a round drum, all the interior oils are pushed through, leaving very little fibre behind.

I have begun with methods of making garlic bread, butter, and croutons, because these appear to be the most popular way of eating garlic. Now, when the cloves are about the size of a thumb, I am giving the amounts in heads of garlic, estimating that there will be about 8 to 12 cloves per head.

Garlic butter
225 g/½ lb salted butter
2 heads of garlic
Juice from 2 lemons
Black pepper

Peel the cloves by scalding, crush the garlic into the lemon juice and discard all the garlic fibre. Heat the lemon and garlic and let it poach gently over a flame for a few minutes. Cool. Have the butter at room temperature so that it is soft, then beat the lemon juice and garlic into the butter so that they are thoroughly mixed together. Return to the refrigerator so that the butter will harden again. It will keep happily for weeks, but cover the bowl, otherwise the refrigerator will stink.

This method avoids melting the butter and cooking the garlic in it, which causes the butter to separate.

167

Garlic bread

Slice a French loaf almost down to the base in 2½ cm/
1 inch pieces, then cover each slice with the garlic
butter, opening the loaf carefully as you go, but being
careful not to break it at the base. Fold the loaf
together again and wrap it in foil, then bake in a
medium oven for about 30 minutes.

Garlic croûtons

Put about a tablespoon of good olive oil into a frying
pan and crush 3 cloves of garlic into it. Take 2 thick
slices of wholemeal bread and cut them into 2½ cm/1
inch squares. Heat the oil and garlic, then fry the
cubes of bread until they are crisp on all their sides
(you must watch and shake the pan). They should
soak up all the oil. I enjoy them most as part of a green
salad. For a soup, most people would dice the bread
smaller, to half the size.

Garlic soup

This is particularly good when you are suffering from
a cold. I once made it out of 250 cloves and the flavour
was not so very different from another soup made out
of 50 cloves. For about 6 people this soup should be
made from 3 heads of garlic which would be roughly
30 cloves.

3 heads of garlic
3 tablespoons olive oil
2 egg yolks

Sauté the peeled garlic cloves in the olive oil in a
saucepan with the lid firmly on for a few minutes, but
gently so that the garlic does not brown or become
crisp. Then add 1100 ml/2 pints of boiling water or
1110 ml/2 pints of vegetable stock, give it a stir and let
it simmer on a modest heat for an hour. Leave to cool.
Add salt and pepper, then blend it all. You will find it

turns to a satisfactory shade of cream. Have your two egg yolks in a mixing bowl and mix the yolks into the soup, then return to the soup in the saucepan and let it thicken a little. It is now ready to serve. It can be garnished with a little chopped mint, parsley, chives or spring onion.

Garlic soup with saffron and potatoes
After blending the garlic and its liquid as in the above recipe, return to the saucepan and add 3 peeled and diced potatoes and the merest pinch of saffron. Simmer for another 20 minutes so that the potatoes are tender.

Garlic soup with poached eggs
After blending the garlic as above, reheat it until just simmering. Carefully break an egg for each person into the soup and poach them. Toast a slice of bread for each egg, put the toast into individual soup bowls, pour the soup over and slide the poached egg on top of the toast. Garnish with chopped parsley and grated parmesan.

Aillade
1 head of garlic
6 fresh tomatoes
Handful of chopped basil
Salt and pepper
140 ml/¼ pint of olive oil

Blend the tomatoes, sieve the liquid, then throw away the bits of skin and pips. Peel the garlic cloves and blend with the tomatoes, basil, salt and pepper, and add the oil. If the sauce is too liquid (it should be like thick pouring cream) add more basil. This is wonderful added at the table to bowls of soup.

LASAGNE VERDE

Pasta served without meat sauce is lighter and more agreeable on the palate. Lasagne tends to be heavy, but when made with vegetable purées it can be almost as buoyant as a soufflé. Spaghetti, fettuccine, tagliatelle, vermicelli are all transformed once you have dumped the bolognese.

I confess I have never made my own pasta. Nor have I been able to enjoy commercial brands which taste of flour mixed with chlorinated tap water. But now on the market, obtainable at wholefood shops, are some delicious types of pasta of high quality (some of the best are imported from Japan) often made from buckwheat.

But the recipe below uses wholewheat lasagne which has thankfully been with us for sometime. A 450 g/1 lb packet holds 25 sheets of pasta. As I estimate the recipe will feed 8 people adequately and you need 10 sheets of pasta, the price is economical. (It is up to you whether the layers of vegetables are separated from each other by pasta. I prefer not to do this, as the lasagne is too heavy, but if this is your inclination, you will need to boil more than 10 sheets of pasta.)

You will need a large pan filled with boiling and lightly salted water. The pasta needs to be boiled for 20 minutes. Do five sheets at a time. If all 10 sheets go in at once, two can stick together and others may stick to the bottom of the pan. Keep a rolling boil going: stronger than a simmer, but not too fierce, or the pasta might tear. When the sheets are done, lift them out with a perforated spoon and let them drain over the colander.

Make the lasagne in a large baking dish — one about 6 to 8 cm/2½ to 3 inches deep and around 25 by 30 cm/10 by 12 inches in size. Le Creuset make a superb rectangular dish 26 by 40 cm/10¼ by 15¾ inches of enamelled cast iron which does wonders for the biceps and the lasagne baked in it. But that size of dish would use double the amounts below.

Pyrex make dishes of about the right size, and an ordinary meat baking dish will do. But whatever the dish, do ensure the base and sides are well oiled or greased. You do not want to leave half of the pasta sticking to the dish when you come to serve it.

Prepare two or three different vegetables for the filling. Vary the texture of the strata by leaving one vegetable finely or coarsely chopped while another is puréed; vary the strata still more by what you add to them: eggs, cream, tofu or different cheeses, a herb sauce or chopped parsley.

The colours can contrast as well. This recipe uses green vegetables, but a proper lasagne verde has spinach added to the pasta. And who cares if your lasagne has the strident vulgarity of a Neapolitan ice cream? We English are too often stifled by the concept of good taste.

Most important of all, the vegetables should be only just cooked, without touching water. They are sautéed in a closed saucepan over a low heat in a tablespoon of olive oil, for only a few minutes, until they have just begun to get soft.

Lasagne Verde
450 g/1 lb leeks
450 g/1 lb courgettes
900 g/2 lb spinach
1 packet of Morinaga tofu
140 ml/¹/₄ pint single cream
2 eggs
4 tablespoons chopped parsley
50 g/2 oz gruyère cheese
100 g/4 oz sage Derby cheese
50 g/2 oz parmesan cheese
25 g/1 oz butter
25 g/1 oz plain flour
275 ml/¹/₂ pint skimmed milk
4 tablespoons skimmed milk powder
10 strips wholewheat cooked lasagne
Olive oil for greasing baking dish and cooking vegetables.

Split the leeks down the centre and wash the earth away. Then slice across in 2.5 cm/1 inch chunks. Use one tablespoon of olive oil at the bottom of the pan. Put the leeks in and the lid on the pan, and leave over a small flame for a few minutes, shaking the pan occasionally to ensure the leeks do not stick or burn. When they have begun to soften, give them a good stir and set aside.

Coarsely chop the spinach and cook in the same way. Slice the courgettes to about $\frac{1}{4}$ cm/$\frac{1}{8}$ inch thickness, and cook in the same way — they will need a minute or two longer.

Oil the baking dish, lay the cooked sheets of lasagne on the base and sides, covering the dish completely so that there is no space between the sheets of pasta. Cover the pasta with the spinach. Drain the packet of tofu and spread over the spinach. Season with sea salt and freshly ground pepper; grate the gruyère and sprinke over the tofu, pressing the layers down so that the top is even. Next, spread the leeks out and season. Then pour the cream over, lay the courgettes over the leeks, season, sprinkle with chopped parsley and pour the beaten egg over the top.

Cover completely with another layer of pasta, then make a roux with the butter and the flour, adding the skimmed milk powder to the skimmed milk to enrich the sauce. Grate the sage Derby and the parmesan into the roux and let the sauce thicken. When the sauce is cool, spoon it over the top of the pasta, making sure there are no bits sticking up out of the sauce. They will blacken and burn, so cut them away.

This lasagne is best left for a day to settle. Then bake in a pre-heated oven, 400°F/205°C/Gas Mark 6, for thirty minutes or until the top is brown and the interior bubbling a little.

CHRISTMAS

From one who dislikes Christmas with Scrooge-like ferocity, here is an alternative to the traditional bird and pud.

I put the four course vegetarian meal below and a two-course traditional Christmas dinner — the menu taken from the Christmas edition of *Woman and Home* — into a computer for analysis. Both meals were calculated for eight people. The results show that the traditional dinner has four times the number of calories (3,000 per person compared with 782 calories in the vegetarian meal). It also has four times the amount of fat, four times the amount of sugar and less than half the dietary fibre.

I tend to begin all dinner parties with a platter of crudités, but it is essential that you have either a home-made mayonnaise or a couple of purées to accompany it. Take trouble over cutting, slicing and arranging the vegetables. Choose the centre hearts of fennel and celery, one green and one red pepper, the flowerets of calabrese and cauliflower, courgettes in julienne strips, tiny mushrooms, curly endive, halved tomatoes covered in pesto sauce (it comes in jars now or make your own, page 136), spring onions, radishes and if you have home-made pickles all the better. The colours can look stunning. Here are the two purées I used.

Spiced avocado purée
2 avocados
2 crushed cloves garlic
140 ml/5 fl oz yoghurt
Juice from 1 lemon
½ teaspoon tabasco sauce
Salt and pepper

Blend all together in a liquidizer to a smooth purée, season with a little salt and black pepper.

Courgette and tofu purée
1 packet Morinago tofu, well drained
170 g/6 oz courgettes, grated
50 g/2 oz curd cheese
1 crushed clove garlic
Little sea salt

Blend all the ingredients together.

Celestial soup
2 heads of celery
2 heads of fennel
1 head of garlic
50 g/2 oz ginger root, unpeeled
2 litres/4 pints water
3 tablespoons natural soy sauce
1 tablespoon sesame oil

Pour boiling water over the cloves of garlic and leave a minute of two to soak. When cool they will peel easily. Wash celery. Chop fennel, unpeeled ginger root, celery and garlic; sauté everything in the sesame oil over a low heat for a few minutes. Add the water. Bring to the boil and let the soup simmer for an hour. Liquidize everything in a blender, then sieve the liquid and throw away all the vegetable debris. Add the soy sauce to the stock.

Keep in the refrigerator for two days. On Christmas morning, heat the soup slowly and let it simmer for 10 minutes before serving. If feeling generous, pour into the soup two or three glasses of dry sherry.

Timbale de crêpes
These are moulded pancakes cooked in a soufflé dish interleaved with various purées and custards. Cook the components separately as follows.

Crêpe batter: (makes 10)
100 g/4 oz plain flour

2 eggs
275 ml/½ pint skimmed milk
3 tablespoons yoghurt
1 teaspoon each salt and garam masala
1 tablespoon sunflower oil

Sift the flour. Beat the eggs into it, and then the rest of the ingredients. Allow the batter to rest for an hour. Oil a pan, heat it, and ladle enough batter into the pan to cover the base with a thin layer. Cook, turn the crêpe, and just let that side dry out before laying the crêpe on a piece of greaseproof paper. Continue until you have used all the batter.

Spinach sauce
450 g/1 lb spinach
25 g/1 oz plain flour
25 g/1 oz butter
2 eggs
50 g/2 oz grated gruyère cheese
Pinch of nutmeg
Sea salt and black pepper

Tear the washed spinach leaves into small pieces, pat them dry in a cloth and place in a saucepan with the butter, nutmeg, salt and pepper. Let the spinach reduce over a low heat for five minutes. Add the flour, stir, then add the cheese. Take away from the heat and when cool beat in the egg.

Mushroom duxelles
450 g/1 lb mushrooms
2 small chopped onions
1 tablespoon olive oil
3 tablespoons chopped parsley

Slice the mushrooms and cook them with the onions in the olive oil. When they start to lose their moisture, raise the heat and stir continuously so that the liquid is evaporated. Watch that they do not burn. They must be cooked and dry. Add a little salt, pepper and the parsley when they are cooked.

Leek custard
450 g/1 lb leeks
1 tablespoon olive oil
1 egg
50 g/2 oz curd cheese

Slice leeks down centre, clean them, and cut them across in 1 cm/¹⁄₂ inch slices. Cook them in the oil over a low heat until they are soft. Allow to cool. Blend in a liquidizer with the cheese and egg and a little salt and pepper.

Butter a 20 cm/8 inch soufflé dish. Take 4 crêpes and arrange them around the sides, allowing 2¹⁄₂ cm/1 inch at the bottom and as much as possible at the top. Place one crêpe at the bottom of the dish and cover with some of the spinach sauce. Place a crêpe over it and add the mushroom duxelles, then another crêpe and the leek custard. You may have room for two or three more layers. Do not feel you have to use up all of the sauces. When the soufflé dish is full, bend over the side crêpes so that they meet at the top and cover with another crêpe.

Put a piece of foil over the top, sit the soufflé dish in a meat tin filled with boiling waer and put into a pre-heated oven 400°F/205°C/Gas Mark 6 for one hour. Take the timbale out of the oven and let it rest for five minutes, then unmould on a hot platter. Serve it by cutting like a cake into wedges.

Accompany the timbale with a tomato or a caper sauce and the traditional — why not? — Brussels sprouts. But do not let them cook for more than three minutes. Directly they all become soft, their flavour radically changes into something quite unpleasant.

I completed this meal with a platter of tropical fruits

around the centre piece of a large pineapple. It is possible to buy — but make sure they are ripe — fresh guavas, lychees, mangoes, passion fruit, papaya or paw paw, even persimmon (Carmel import them as Sharon fruit).

VEGETARIANS' CHOICE

Crudités
with
Avocado and tofu purées

Celestial soup

Timbale de crêpes
with
Caper sauce and Brussels sprouts

Tropical fruits

TRADITIONAL MENU

Roast Turkey
with
Lemon and parsley stuffing

Roast potatoes, bread sauce

Chipolata sausages

Brussels sprouts with chestnuts

Christmas pudding with brandy butter

Index

179